Overcoming Imposter Syndrome:
Unlock Your True Potential So You Can Thrive in Life

YOU ARE NOT

AN

IMPOSTER

COLINE MONSARRAT

Edited by Quinn Courtwright
Cover art by Miladinka Milic

Published by Apicem Publishing
www.apicempublishing.com

APICEM PUBLISHING

Apicem Publishing
1309 Coffeen Avenue STE 1200
Sheridan, WY 82801, United States

ISBN:
Paperback: 978-1-959814-02-3
Hardback: 978-1-959814-03-0

First Published in 2023.

To my mother, who gave me unconditional love and support

To Aurore, to whom I will be forever grateful

To all the persons who still need to break their mask

CONTENTS

YOU ARE NOT AN IMPOSTER

"When you change your thoughts, remember to also change your world."

\- Norman Vincent Peale

PREFACE

An autumn day in 1997 in my childhood bedroom.

"Coline, you do not have to lie if you do not want to go to school."

These few words pronounced by my mother when I was 6 years old, as insignificant as they were, would later trigger my impostor syndrome. A syndrome that could have sent me straight to the cemetery without the intervention of one of my closest friends. A syndrome that gradually infiltrated all parts of my life until it dictated a large part of my actions, much to my dismay. It took me 23 years to understand the causes and, above all, to overcome it. Twenty-three years of lacking self-confidence, sabotage, people pleasing, and many other attitudes that I didn't even realize to what extent they were running my life.

But sometimes life is good when you look at the events that happen to you in a certain way. I had to experience a brush with death to finally understand this lesson. The day of January 3, 2020 will remain forever engraved in my memory. This day changed my life forever. My entourage and the people who witnessed the events that happened to me find me unlucky. But on the contrary, I am one of the luckiest people on this earth. Thanks to this event, I finally freed myself from a syndrome that kept me locked up and prevented me from living my life entirely.

It took me more than a year and a half to understand how beliefs built in childhood and became deeply engraved in my subconscious held me captive. But today, as I write these words, I am proud to say that I have finally removed my mask of the impostor.

In writing this book, I aim to help you become aware of how your beliefs and thinking patterns influence your daily actions and prevent you from reaching your greatest potential. By telling you my story and the actions I took to free myself from this damn syndrome, I hope you, too, will take the steps to drop your mask.

INTRODUCTION

My imposter syndrome began when I was just a little girl. It started in one part of my life but quickly infiltrated every part of my being. It was not until I reached 30 years old that I understood what imposter syndrome was and how it dictated my life. I want to be straight: I believe that a small pinch of imposter syndrome can actually benefit you in life. Indeed, it makes you want to grow, and it challenges you to want to become a better person.

However, it is when the syndrome becomes too prominent that it becomes dangerous. When the tumor is too large, it starts to affect your life negatively and stops you from living it to the fullest. This is when it becomes crucial to take action to try to eradicate it. Because if you do not, it invades your subconscious brain and slowly starts to affect all areas of your life. In the best-case scenario, it would be beneficial to try to eradicate it before it becomes tumor sized. However, if you are as stubborn as me, you usually need a slap in the face before you take action.

We mostly know imposter syndrome at work as it is indeed highly felt and more visible in professional settings. It is the area on which most psychology research about imposter syndrome has focused. It does not take much retrospection to realize that you are a victim of it at work.

My first realization about feeling like an imposter also came from my behaviors at work. It was only later that I realized the roots of it and how it had spread into my life. According to Robinson (2017), imposter syndrome is "a pervasive feeling of self-doubt, insecurity, and incompetence despite evidence that you are skilled and successful" (para. 1). In other words, as a person living with imposter syndrome, you believe that your success is the result of external factors and that you do not deserve the recognition. You constantly fear being found out that you are not the person everyone else thinks you are. The syndrome rests on this one distorted belief but impacts all spheres of a person's life. We must admit that it is a heavy mask to wear.

It is estimated that 70% of all people suffer from imposter syndrome at some point in their lives. Therefore, we can conclude that it seems to be an epidemic and one that has been part of human life for quite some time. However, it was not until 1978 that imposter syndrome was conceptualized by two psychologists, Pauline Rose Clance and Suzanne Imes (1978), in "The Imposter

Phenomenon in High Achieving Women: Dynamics and Therapeutic Intervention." Their study began with the theory that the "imposter phenomenon," as they called it back then, was mostly affecting high-achieving females. To test their theory, the two psychologists studied groups of successful women from various fields.

They found that despite their accomplishments, these women still felt like imposters, like they were not supposed to be where they were, and that they had gotten there through dumb luck or by fooling others into thinking they were more intelligent than they actually were.

Interestingly, the study found that the majority of these women had internalized messages from their parents or other authority figures early in life that intelligence was something one was born with and not something that could be developed. This message led them to believe that they could not get better at things, which in turn made them more likely to attribute their success to external factors instead of their own abilities. The findings in this study teaches you something crucial about this syndrome: It shows us the impact of early childhood on the development of our embedded beliefs.

If you really start screening your life, you will realize that it has spread into all aspects of your existence. You feel like an imposter in your relationships, as a parent, and even with your health. But do you understand this cost? Most likely, you have not realized it. You are so used to acting the way you do that it becomes normal behavior.

The mask has become your second skin and gives you a sense of security. In the end, you are just a fraud waiting to be found out. At least, that's what you believe, and that's what I thought, too.

Before we move further in discovering imposter syndrome, I would like to highlight an important fact: Originally, impostor syndrome was formerly thought to be a trait that was only typical of high-achieving women. Even today, when we talk about imposter syndrome, we often refer to women having it rather than men. However, additional studies have demonstrated that it affects both men and women, collectively speaking, in that the proportions affected are more or less divided evenly among the sexes.

So why do we tend to think that women are the most affected? In my opinion, the reason is simple: Men are less likely to admit that they are suffering from this syndrome due to the pressure of social norms. We cannot deny that society (and sometimes us without realizing it) tells men that to be "real" men, they should be strong and confident. In my opinion, the rising mental health issues faced by some men nowadays due to the heavy loads of stereotypes are a big problem that should be addressed, but this subject deserves a book on its own, and it is not mine to write.

Although imposter syndrome is not an official psychiatric diagnosis, the impact is widely recognized by psychiatrists, psychologists, and counselors who have to assist people like us who believe that they are imposters in their own lives. Even though it affects many people, the syndrome is still seen as taboo. It can be tricky to realize that we are victims of this phenomenon as imposter syndrome usually comes with low self-esteem and lack of confidence. I am sure that as you read this book, the feeling of shame will invade you many times as your brain tells you what a fraud you are.

It doesn't matter if you're tired of always agreeing to do things you don't want to do, if you'll accept anything to prove that you're capable even if you don't believe it yourself, or if a comment that wasn't even aimed at you in the first place sends you into torment for days. Your mask is so tight that it blinds you to the fact that these thoughts are unfounded and that you are a victim of being tricked by your brain.

But here is the good news: If you decide to take action and start a journey into self-discovery (as painful as it can be, at least for me, it was), you too can crack your mask and let your true self shine. I am not going to lie: It is not an easy and quick journey. But it might be one of the most important ones you take.

Humans love to blame others or external factors for what happens to us. When in fact, we are mostly responsible for how our lives unfold and our choices. If there is one thing I have learned and lived by ever since these events, it is that I am the author of my life. It is tough for us to understand that life is not fair (a concept that is important to most of us) and that, in fact, we are entitled to nothing. But once we understand this, it becomes easier to adapt ourselves so we can make better choices and decisions. It can also push us to act. If I hadn't lived all of it, I would still be walking with my mask on and be limited by my distorted beliefs. We are the sole owner of our lives, and I truly believe how we look at and react to situations will determine our quality of life.

You might feel ashamed as you realize how your beliefs and your behaviors made you fall into this rabbit hole. At least I was. I am not proud to say that I had to go through the loss of an organ to realize how I had been sabotaging myself for decades. This journey was not easy. I had to face the harsh truth of how I had deliberately placed myself in these situations.

During my journey, I have cried, faced regrets, and felt angry about how stupid I had been, to name a few difficult moments. But none of these feelings can counter the laughter, peace, and pride that these events have brought me. If there is one piece of advice to give you as you start your own journey, it is to stop lying to yourself and examine yourself as an outsider. Don't be afraid of what you will find and realize along the way as this self-awareness will set you free.

My fight against imposter syndrome started against my will in January 2020. The events that took place back then forced me to look for answers. I had reached such a high level within the spectrum of imposter syndrome that my life depended on confronting it. I had to change if I did not want to have my name written on a stone.

It took me almost two years to understand how I

ended up in these situations. How a simple sentence said to me when I was a child fostered a belief that would almost kill me decades later. I quickly became aware of my irrationality. I knew something was wrong with my thinking patterns and behaviors, but it took me time to understand the roots and how they had impacted my life.

When the first events of 2020 happened, I had only one question: How the heck did I end up in this situation? I wanted so much to understand how I came to be the person I was that I went back to study psychology at a university. The idea of finding the answers consumed me. This book retraces my journey and how, step-by-step, I have turned my life around.

As you read these words, I can only imagine your eyes rolling while thinking about the time it took me. You have picked up a book on how to conquer imposter syndrome and intend to fix it as fast as it takes a rocket to reach space. In the end, you have already realized that imposter syndrome has been affecting your life for many years, and you have no time to waste.

I understand you as I was the same. We all want a quick fix for everything. Industries have made billions using these false beliefs that we can change everything we want at the click of a button or by popping something out of a box. We do not have time to be patient. We want everything now. But I am sorry to break it to you: No great things in life come easily. Real change takes time and effort.

But I was like you. Once I became conscious of the

problem, I had no time to wait, and the faster I fixed it, the better it would be. However, even if I hated this idea, I had to learn the virtuous concept of patience. Many times during this two-year journey, I thought I was finally free. I thought I would solve all my 25 years' worth of psychological distortion in the space of a month. I was foolish. And if I had continued believing as I did, I would not be where I am today.

What would you think if someone came to you tomorrow and said they could take a pill and lose all their extra weight in a day without any effort? You would just think that they were nuts. So use the same thinking patterns when thinking about yourself. Instead of blaming yourself for taking a long time to do anything in life, whether it is losing weight or fighting the imposter inside you, look back at everything you have accomplished and enjoy the ride.

What I have learned during my journey is that it is actually a combination of mental patterns that group together to form the imposter syndrome. By debunking each of them, one after the other, you will be able to break them, so you can finally thrive in your life.

I do not think you can—or should—completely eradicate imposter syndrome. A small pinch of imposter syndrome can help you take action and help you grow. Imagine if you were entirely sure of everything you did: You would likely miss any warning signs and just head straight into a wall. But having a little bit of imposter syndrome and being a victim of it are very different things. You need to readjust your place on the spectrum to find the balance.

But please promise me something: Don't be as stubborn as I was.

It's never too late to be your true self; believe me, that's one of the best journeys you will ever take.

PART ONE

The Imposter Mask

1.

The Consequences of Imposter Syndrome

"Sometimes you aren't listening to your body because you're listening to everybody else's expectations."

- Ann Voskamp

January 2020

I had relocated to Dubai four years earlier to take on my dream job. The city was full of opportunities, and I was ready to seize them. In my mind, life was going well except for chronic fatigue, which had afflicted me for a few years. It was causing me to be very emotional, and as a person with difficulty dealing with emotions, this fatigue was a problem I wished to solve.

Unfortunately for me, nobody understood my concerns as I was, for them, one of the most dynamic people they knew. Doctors did not find anything wrong, and I even had a pharmacist tell me one day that if *I* needed vitamins, what would other people even need? So I buried my intuition of there being something wrong with me, moved on with my life, and continued ignoring the signals my body was sending me.

It was January 3rd, and the mild sunshine illuminated Dubai at the beginning of the year and predicted a good day. The new year promised a good year ahead, and I had spent the day before writing down my new resolution and goals for 2020, my lucky number as well. Finally, I was sure of something: 2020 would be one of the best years of my life. I was right, but not in the sense I thought.

As a 29-year-old, I was full of dreams and did not doubt their realizations. They were typical for my age: reach a new milestone in my career, get in better shape (I must say, that might be the only one I achieved), and find love, to name a few. So, as I finished my list and set down my pen, I cheered to the new year with a smile on my face.

The weather was beautiful, so I planned to meet my friends at a beach restaurant for lunch. A nice dish and a glass of rosé in good company under the sun—what more could a person want? At that moment, I thought I was very lucky to be able to live this life.

We had finished eating, and I stayed at the restaurant with my friend Kayleigh while the guys went on to play soccer. Suddenly, a cold wave came over me. It was 75 degrees outside, but I felt like I was lying in the snow. I had no idea what was going on. As an attempt to warm up, I ordered a coffee and borrowed my friend's jacket. But nothing worked. It became increasingly complicated for me to focus on the conversation as I had only one wish: to go back home and sneak into my bed.

The problem was that, as a people pleaser, it was inconceivable for me to abandon my friend alone in the restaurant. My own feelings of discomfort were not enough of a good reason. As she talked, keeping my eyes open and controlling my shivering became harder. I sat in misery, trying my best to control my body for more than an hour before finally getting up the nerve to say that it was best for me to go home. As soon as the guys returned, I seized the opportunity to leave while reassuring them that I must just be tired, and a nap would put me back on my feet. We had planned to go out in the evening, and I was convinced I would be able to go.

The taxi ride home made me feel even more like a fraud. My driver was from Pakistan. As soon as he saw me shivering, he turned on the car heater to its maximum, so I could warm up. Drops of sweat were falling down his face due to the heat of the car. As I thanked him for his gesture, he started telling me that he understood what it meant to be fighting coldness. At that very moment, his wife and three children were walking across Pakistan toward his brother's house as his house did not have a heating system, and it was snowing. It would be a three day walk before they arrived.

You can imagine how ashamed I was; me, a 29-year-old French woman who was comfortably living in a nice apartment in the center of Dubai, shivering in the back seat of his taxi. I belonged to the lucky group.

After a 20-minute ride under tropical conditions for him and the north pole for me, I arrived home and ran into my bed. As my eyes closed, I thought of how much better I would be once I had slept a bit.

Unfortunately, things did not go as planned. When I woke up a few hours later, I had sweat so much that I looked like I had just gotten out of the shower. The fever was rising and continued to grow for the next three days. You would think that I would have gone to see a doctor during this time. But why would I do that? For me, it was just a cold. I had nothing worth disturbing a doctor for. On the third day, I decided to go for a walk to try to get better. I thought that walking was always a good idea when you caught a cold. It would help me get back in shape so that I could start my workweek fresh and in shape.

The fever hadn't gone down when I woke up on Sunday morning. Unfortunately for me, the workweek was starting, and I could not conceive of missing a workday because of a cold. I needed to gather my strength and keep going. As I was taking my shower, I could feel the tap water mixed with the fever's sweat dripping down my body. I kept repeating to myself, "This is nothing, Coline. It's just a cold."

When I arrived at work, my manager Aurore, who is like a mother to me, immediately asked me to go home and consult with a doctor. I was drenched in sweat, and she feared a flu epidemic. You should have seen my face when she mentioned that I could have the flu. I was in total shock. Me? Have the flu? No way; people who have the flu are really sick, while I am not.

The feeling of guilt that came over me was even more challenging to deal with than the fever. I couldn't help but think that I was making a fuss and that, soon enough, they would realize I had nothing. My heart was pounding as these thoughts invaded my brain. I returned home feeling like a fraud who would soon be discovered.

During the afternoon, she told me she would come to pick me up at the end of the day to drive me to the emergency room. I strictly refused and said that I would be back at work the next day. Going to the hospital was impossible for me. Only people who are truly sick go there. But she was there at 7 p.m. to drag me despite my refusal and unwillingness.

You have to give her credit for her perseverance, and for the rest of my life, I will forever be grateful for it.

On the way to the hospital, I couldn't help but think what a fraud I was. As you may know, that feeling of guilt eats you away on the inside. It makes you tremble and paralyzed in fear. At that moment, thousands of thoughts were clashing in my head. I could barely stay still in the car seat as I thought about how I deceived her when she found out that it was just a fuss over nothing. As we arrived at the ER, the imposter in me saw this dreadful moment finally arrive.

And that was exactly what happened when we arrived —when we checked in, the nurses looked at me as if I had nothing wrong. I had taken painkillers a few hours earlier to decrease the fever. I did not look very sick to them. Their behaviors supported my beliefs, and I was then begging to go home.

They still decided to do routine blood tests as we were

already there. As I sat in the waiting room next to Aurore, the fever started to rise again. It might sound ridiculous, but I began to feel happy about it. I needed proof of my legitimacy of being in this hospital.

As I started to shiver, the nurse came running back to see me. Their faces and behaviors had changed. It turned out it wasn't a cold; I had sepsis and was entering sepsis shock. This result should have validated that I was experiencing something severe, but for me, it did not. I still believed that I had nothing more than a cold; they were wrong and would soon realize their mistakes.

Self-Awareness: Why It's Both Challenging and Essential

You see, the problem with being an imposter is that this feeling of fraud leads you to an overwhelming feeling of shame. How can you dare to complain? You invalidate your emotions because you believe that you do not deserve them. That they are unfounded. At that moment, you just want to disappear as the shame is too strong.

According to psychologists, it is easy for our brain to invalidate our feelings. It is a defense mechanism to protect our ego and self-esteem. But by invalidating our emotions, we are not allowing ourselves to heal and grow. I wish I understood that it was okay to feel what I felt, even if it may have seemed irrational or unfounded.

As an outsider, you might wonder how I could have been that stupid, whereas the imposter inside you does the exact same thing. How often does someone need to tell you that you are amazing at your work or as a parent? But do you believe them? No, you don't. Your beliefs are so ingrained that you invalidate their compliments, keep believing that they are wrong, and worry they will find out soon that you are right about being inadequate. Trust me, I understand how we love to be right, but in this case, it has a dreadful impact on our lives.

Moreover, as humans, we always look for evidence that will support our beliefs. Many studies have shown that we tend to remember information that confirms our beliefs and forget information that contradicts them. This is called confirmation bias, which is one of the main reasons impostor syndrome persists. We only look for evidence that supports our belief that we're not good enough or a fraud soon to be discovered and ignore all the evidence to the contrary.

It is easier to realize it when you look at it from the outside. We are very good at analyzing our friends and talking about how they lack self-awareness. But when it comes to ourselves, we forget everything that we preach. This is why, exactly like you, I could not see how irrational and foolish I was. I only realized when it was too late. I also had to face the harsh truth surrounding this syndrome: how costly it can be.

One of the first steps in my journey was to become self-aware. To be honest, as you will see later, I had no choice but to admit that this syndrome had caused me great loss. But instead of denying this fact, I decided that I would not let my beliefs destroy me and risk affecting my future to an even greater degree.

It is almost impossible for someone with imposter syndrome to accept that they can be loved and appreciated for their authentic self. The need in your mind to keep up the appearance of being successful causes constant psychological distress. The problem is that until you realize this, you will most likely keep going as I did.

So why is it so difficult for us to be self-aware? One reason could be that we are so caught up in our own thoughts and perspectives that it's hard to step back and see ourselves objectively. We are experts at seeing others for who they are, but we cannot see ourselves clearly. As I researched to respond to this question, I found a study published in *Harvard Business Review* that showed that in the workplace, while 95% of people believed they were self-aware, only 10–15% actually were (Eurich, 2018). That number is staggering.

This lack of self-awareness can have serious consequences, both personally and professionally:

- It can lead to problems in relationships.
- It becomes difficult to understand and communicate effectively with others if we don't truly know ourselves.
- It can hinder our career growth as we may not understand our strengths and weaknesses.
- It can lead us to make poor decisions or miss out on opportunities.

Another factor preventing self-awareness could be fear—we may not want to face uncomfortable truths about ourselves or acknowledge our flaws. I was a victim of that for sure.

How to Cultivate Self-Awareness

I decided to try to learn more about our subconscious and how it works. That's when I came across the book, *Your Subconscious Brain can Change Your Life*.

In his book, Dow (2019) explains how our beliefs are engraved in our subconscious and how difficult it is to change them. Our subconscious often gets in the way when we try to do something new or different. It's like imposter syndrome where we doubt ourselves and our abilities. Dow says that to change our beliefs, we first need to be aware of them. Once we're aware of them, we can begin to question, and eventually change, them.

I realized that I was completely lacking self-awareness and decided to try to change this first using the following practices:

- **Belief change exercise**: In this exercise, you write down a belief that you have about yourself, such as "I'm not good enough." Then, you write down evidence that contradicts that belief. For example, "I've been successful in the past, so I must be good enough." Finally, you write down a new belief that you want to have about yourself, such as "I am good enough." By doing this exercise, you can begin to change your beliefs which will lead you down the road to success.

- **Introspection and reflection**: Take time each day to consider your thoughts, feelings, and actions. Ask yourself why you made certain choices or reacted in a particular way. This practice can help uncover underlying beliefs and patterns that may be holding you back.

- **Seek feedback from others**: Do not be afraid to seek feedback from others as it can be so valuable. Ask trusted friends and colleagues for their honest opinions on your strengths and weaknesses. This outside perspective can provide valuable insight into how you are perceived by others and areas where you may need improvement. It is also important to be open to learning and growth. Don't become defensive or shut down when receiving criticism or constructive feedback. Instead, consider it as an opportunity for personal development and use it to make positive changes in your behavior.

- **Practice mindfulness**: This involves being present in the moment and observing your thoughts and emotions without judgment. Mindfulness techniques such as meditation

can help improve awareness of yourself and
the world around you.

The Cost of Imposter Syndrome at Work

As mentioned earlier, my imposter syndrome was the
most visible at work. And most victims of imposter
syndrome only realize that they are suffering from these
debilitating thoughts when thinking about the workplace.
At least until they decide to look at their behaviors in the
other areas of their lives.

As an imposter, you believe that you do not deserve
your job despite your achievements and the validation of
your colleagues. Let me describe your attitude at work: I
am pretty sure that if I go to your workplace in the early
morning or late evening, I will find you at your desk
trying to complete every task to the highest standard.
Even small and tiny mistakes can set you into panic mode
and make you feel as if you have let everyone down. You
watch your colleagues and friends with envy as they seem
to have everything under control when your life is chaotic.

Let me reassure you: I am not a psychic, and I have
not been spying on you. What I have described above are
the usual patterns that consume people with imposter
syndrome. I have to say that it could be my autobiogra-
phy, as yours, I am sure. I have merely studied them and
laughed at how real they are.

Your imposter feelings may be sabotaging your
success. Your fear of failure may keep you from taking

risks, voicing opinions, and volunteering for projects—all necessary to climb the ladder of promotion.

Being scared of failure also leads to avoiding big projects in favor of menial tasks. Soon your manager will avoid involving you as you seem to be too busy with insignificant work to be interested in collaborating on big projects.

Another way in which you can sabotage your success is by not having an opinion when asked for one. If you do not think your opinion is worth sharing, others will soon stop asking for it. How can a manager believe in you and trust you with important work if you don't believe in yourself?

Workaholism

The irony is that when we suffer from imposter syndrome, we tend to be perfectionists and driven to succeed. However, this success starts the distorted imposter thoughts, leading to more hard work, more success, and an even greater feeling of being an imposter.

Many imposter syndrome victims do not believe they deserve the job they have or the achievements they get praised for. They believe it was all a "lucky" coincidence, and they need to prove themselves (or so they think) by working harder than anyone else. This habit of "over-working" quickly leads to full-blown workaholism.

Although the term *workaholism* has been in use since the 1970s, researchers and psychologists cannot agree on what it should encompass or if it should be a disorder at all. What they do agree on is that one can become so fixated on one's work that it looks like an addiction. The motivation for this addiction may differ from person to person, but the outcome stays the same.

We all have to work long hours, or over weekends on occasion, but this does not make us workaholics. You may admit that you overwork or even that you are a workaholic, but you may not realize the high price you are paying for trying to prove yourself in this way.

I was one of these people. And even though I am still a workaholic today, the reasons and motives behind it are very different than before. My passion is now my work when before, overworking was a coping mechanism for the imposter in me.

I was shocked when I read for the first time the term *karoshi*. It is a term in the Japanese culture for death due to overwork. Many people work more than 70 hours a week in Japan; this is seen as "normal" and honorable. There are an estimated 10,000 deaths per year from this practice, either from dying as a direct result of overwork or people committing suicide as they can no longer bear the work pressure (Fuerte, 2021). As I read the stories of 40–50-year-old men who collapsed from heart attacks due to overworking, I was shocked. Was it worth it?

Today, we need to face the fact that *karoshi* is no longer a Japanese problem, but a global one. According to a 2016 report by the World Health Organization, long working hours are directly linked to an increase in deaths from heart disease and stroke (as cited in Fuerte, 2021).

I will not lie; this fact did not sit well with me as I have worked with passion since I started my career. But what was the reason for my workaholism? Was I working so hard because I was passionate about my job or to prove something? Knowing the reasons might sound like a waste of time for some, but for me, it was not. Because if you work for passion, chances are you will not develop resentment and frustration. However, if your workaholism is a coping mechanism in an attempt to compensate, the outcome will be more detrimental.

Physical, Mental, and Emotional Costs

You may admit that you overwork or even that you are a workaholic, but you may not realize the high price you are paying for trying to prove yourself in this way.

For example, being a complete workaholic, I have developed trouble sleeping which I now know has greatly affected my health. I could never really "switch off" and slept badly as a result. This vicious cycle is stimulated by the body's production of cortisol (the stress hormone) due to work stress. Cortisol inhibits the production of melatonin (the sleep hormone), making it difficult to sleep. This leads to more stress because of sleep deprivation and more cortisol being produced. When I now think about those sleepless nights, I must admit that they were not worth it.

Apart from the physical and mental consequences of overworking, the toll on relationships is high. If you have a family, chances are that you spend so much time at work that your spouse can feel disconnected. And when your spouse addresses the problem of overworking, it is met with anger and hostility. Your spouse knows that they are playing second fiddle and may start to disengage from the relationship. You are so busy with work-related responsibilities that you neglect your responsibilities at home, leading to resentment from your partner. You may feel entitled and expect your partner to cater to your needs as you are "working so hard." The issue is that we only look at situations from our own perspectives. We fail to put ourselves in others' shoes and see how our actions impact them.

We forget to see that our spouse or partner may feel that their emotional well-being is not important to us, resulting in a lack of trust, respect, and friendship. When this happens, the relationship is in real danger of breaking up. We are so caught up in our quest to prove ourselves and our worthiness that we neglect to see how much it costs us.

But the price gets even higher when you have children. A workaholic is by definition an absent parent. They may be telling themselves that they are working so hard to provide for their families, but in truth, they are working to feel better about themselves, and in the process, damaging the relationship with their children. The children of a workaholic parent will feel that they are unimportant as the parent continuously chooses work over them. As their emotional needs are not met by the absent parent, the children of a workaholic are more likely to suffer from depression and other mental problems.

When workaholism affects only ourselves, we could say that it is only a question of us accepting the price. For example, I could clearly see my workaholism was affecting my health but decided to keep going as it was only impacting me. Additionally, I thought that I was ready to pay the price of its consequences, which was truly short-sighted as that is easier to say when everything is fine.

But what I failed to see was how my family would feel if something bad happened to me. We often like to proclaim when we make a bad decision that it is our problem so only we should decide. But that is only true if you are completely alone in your life, which is most likely not the case.

I thought I was invincible. I did not clearly realize the price we pay for our actions until it was too late. So let me ask you, how much are you willing to lose before you act? Sadly, I am not proud to say, I was willing to lose a lot.

The Cost Increases Exponentially

January 2020

Based on the results that revealed I was going into sepsis shock, the doctor immediately suspected a kidney problem. On January 8th, he advised that I undergo an

MRI in an emergency, as was the case; the outlook of the situation did not look good for me.

I was still in complete denial, so I was not very fond of the idea and did not see the point. This was without counting on the tenacity of Aurore, who did not intend to give up. Living in a country where the medical world is a business, Aurore went on to fight with the insurance company to get everything approved, letting me stew on my emergency bed, feeling more and more like a fraud. When the insurance refused the MRI, it validated my thoughts that I had nothing worth investigating.

I denied the doctor's request to be hospitalized and receive antibiotics, begging to go home. I confess that Aurore only conceded to my request because I lied to her: I promised I would go to another hospital the next day to receive the needed antibiotics.

The following month was one of the hardest of my life. Of course, the sepsis continued to progress due to my inactivity, and when I finally decided that it was time to go back to the hospital, things were not looking that great for me. The insurance finally accepted the MRI request, and it turned out that the doctor at the first hospital was right. One of my kidneys was blocked by a stone that caused the infection to spread like a wildfire.

The fatigue I had been living with for years was, in fact, real. I came to find out that I had been living with only one functioning kidney for years. A mixed feeling invaded me when I heard the news: On one hand, I felt relief at the sound of this validation, and on the other hand, I got angry with myself for having to reach this level to realize that something was wrong. There is a level of blindness that truly makes you feel stupid.

Unfortunately for me, the price to pay would be higher than I thought. My kidney issue was just the tip of the iceberg.

I will always remember the day I stormed into Aurore's office before I even knew what would unravel next. I just told her, "I am grateful I do not have any health issues. I am such a wimp!"

I can imagine how the universe must have laughed sarcastically at that moment.

Outside of making you feel like crap, imposter syndrome has a price. Depending on the spectrum where you fall, this price will change. However, there is something I can guarantee you: The more you wait to fix it, the higher the price will be.

As you are reading the book, you might not yet have realized how much you paid for living with this syndrome. It is hard to measure when you have lived like this for so long, especially if you have lacked self-awareness. It can also be difficult to try to calculate it:

- How many opportunities did you lose?
- How did it impact your health and well-being?
- What else did you lose due to the syndrome?

However, there are moments when the cost of it

becomes so high that you have no choice but to act. It was in my case. I had lived with it for decades without addressing it or even realizing having it until it almost cost me my life. I did not realize I was losing money, as my syndrome stopped me from asking for a salary increase. I did not realize how trying to please everyone so they would not discover that I was a fraud affected my health. I did not realize how hiding behind perfectionism stopped me from going after bigger goals. No, I did not. And I did not even recognize it after that day in the emergency room. It was only when I had lost much more that I finally opened my eyes.

Three weeks after the beginning of the sepsis, I was scheduled for the first surgery to attempt to clear the infection. Breaking the stone with a shockwave operation was too risky, my doctor said. The waves could spread the infection further, leading to a higher risk of death. The only solution was to drain the kidney first before breaking the stone. I went to this surgery with a smile on my face, thinking that soon, everything would be over.

Unfortunately, it did not go as planned. The stone was completely blocking the ureter, making it impossible for the surgeon's team to insert a tube to empty the kidney. When I opened my eyes, I was left in confusion as I learned what had happened.

I had no choice but to move on to the second surgery: break the stone with the shockwave. I must admit that this time the imposter syndrome helped me. I was still in complete denial of the extent of the issue and, therefore, could not imagine the risk I was facing. Two days later, I checked in at the hospital and laughed with the nurses over how silly I had been as I went inside the operating theater.

Luck struck again for me: The surgery went very well, and to my doctor's biggest surprise, I regained perfect kidney function. I was very fortunate. The story could have ended there. But life decided to make me really understand a lesson. In fact, as I would come to realize, this episode was only the beginning. You see, I am a very stubborn person. It is one of my biggest flaws. And that might be why the universe decided to ensure I learned my lessons thoroughly.

And it was right. I needed to go through all of it to finally understand how my thought patterns affected my behaviors and how I viewed life.

In less than two years, I underwent eight surgeries and lost an organ due to my imposter syndrome. But most importantly, I would also finally eliminate it.

The Neuroscience of It All

When reflecting on these events, I wondered why it seems like we must face real adversity before taking action. We often hear stories of how someone turned their life around when they reached rock bottom. I was clearly in this situation. Can we motivate ourselves to change before we pay the highest price for our mistakes?

According to research in neuroscience, our brains are

wired to prioritize immediate rewards over long-term benefits. This means that we often choose the quick and easy solution, even if it may result in negative consequences down the road. In addition, the brain's prefrontal cortex, responsible for controlling impulses and making long-term decisions, is not fully developed until our mid-20s.

This explains why it may take hitting a low point before we are able to make positive changes in our lives. The immediate reward of staying in our comfort zone can be hard to resist, but once we experience the negative consequences, the long-term benefits of change become more appealing.

However, this does not mean that we can't motivate ourselves to make positive changes before reaching a crisis point, thankfully. By actively working on improving self-control and decision-making skills, we can override our brain's natural tendencies and create lasting change in our lives. So while it may be easier said than done, it is possible to break this pattern and prevent ourselves from hitting rock bottom.

Of course, this realization did not immediately come to me, as you will see. It took time, effort, and big losses to break old patterns and establish new, healthier ones. But by understanding the science behind why we may need to hit a low point before making changes, I was able to actively work toward improving my life before it spiraled out of control again.

2.

Understanding the Roots of Imposter Syndrome

"Man is what he believes."

- Anton Chekhov

T he impact of imposter syndrome on your life can be powerful, and you may be paying a high price, as we have seen. But where does it come from? I firmly believe that to fix any situation in life, we must understand the root of the problem, as failing to do so may lead to only patching it up. If you only fix the symptoms, you are just putting a bandage over it, leaving the scars behind it unhealed.

So I tried to understand where my imposter syndrome was coming from, and here is what I found out.

The Impact of Our Childhood

What I came to learn is that imposter syndrome usually erupts in childhood without us even realizing it. As humans, our early experiences in life have a massive impact on our adult behaviors and beliefs. We learn from these experiences, and they shape how we see the world. As we grow into adulthood, we build schemata based on our experiences. Schemata are basically mental models that we use to organize and make sense of our experiences. We use them to predict what will happen next, and they guide our behavior.

Most of the time, schemata are helpful. They help us navigate the world and make sense of what's happening around us. But sometimes, they can lead us astray. This is the case for the ones that lead to imposter syndrome.

By understanding the roots of things, we can slowly start to deconstruct them and change so we can heal. So as painful as it was, I immersed myself in my memories to analyze them in order to find the cause of my impostor syndrome. And the roots quickly surfaced.

Little Coline, Big Problems

The beliefs that made me develop imposter syndrome came from one event, and more particularly, one sentence, that was said to me when I was six years old. However, my imposter syndrome started a year prior, erupting in one part of my life to spread slowly in the others.

At five years old, I started to get sick on a regular basis. I would suddenly have a sharp and excruciating pain starting in my stomach and quickly spreading to my entire body. The pain was so strong that it inhibited walking, eating, drinking, and even thinking for days. Only the long hours inside a burning bath helped release some of the pain.

When it first happened, my parents were a little bit puzzled as they saw me crying for help. In the end, I was only five years old, and it is common to assume that kids have a higher tendency for drama. My general practitioner reassured my mother and diagnosed me with no more than a stomach bug. Nothing out of the ordinary for a child.

The second time I got sick, things were a little bit more suspicious for my parents and doctor. I was not showcasing the normal symptoms of a stomach bug: I did not need to vomit and none of my siblings were affected by this condition known to be highly contagious. This was when it got complicated for me.

Even if I could not comprehend everything as I was so young; I still remember how I realized that trust surrounding whether I was really sick was a question in my mother's eyes.

In 1997, I was six and ready to start elementary school. I loved going to school. Even if my high level of energy was sometimes difficult to manage (especially for my teacher), I was full of life and passionate about learning new things. I always went to school with a smile on my face.

Autumn had only started when my freedom was ripped away once more. I woke up with a stabbing pain—again. Tears started to drain down my face as I realized that I would lose my ability to do the things I loved, like school, for the next week at the bare minimum. I was crying so loudly that my mother came to my bed to see what was happening. I could hardly tell her how much I was suffering as the pain was so unbearable. She left me in my bed resting to go and manage my brother and sister, who were preparing to go to school. We are all one and a half years apart, so I'll let you imagine the workload it was to handle us.

When she returned home, I still had not been showing any normal symptoms from a stomach bug outside of the pain, which was hard for her to measure (even so for professionals). And that's when it happened: I could not stop my tears as I heard the words, "Coline, you do not have to lie if you do not want to go to school." That's when my mother started to think that I was lying. This is a memory that has haunted me for decades, deeply buried in my subconscious.

I was torn between the pain and the feeling of disappointing the most important person in my life. I had no way to prove my statements, and I started to doubt my own pain. Maybe I was weaker than the other kids. Why was I not able to run as they did when they had a stomach bug? Why was I different?

The feeling of shame and weakness started to build in me. It would become a big part of my personality. And with this event, slowly, I started to develop all the symptoms that compose imposter syndrome: self-doubt, lack of confidence, low self-esteem, perfectionism, people pleasing, and a feeling of being a fraud.

These symptoms would follow me throughout my life, impacting every area. I would doubt my abilities and accomplishments, always feeling like a fraud, no matter how much evidence I had to the contrary. I would people-please and put others' needs before my own in an attempt to prove my worthiness, and I would second-guess everything I did, always assuming that I was wrong. Imposter syndrome would become my constant companion, and it would take me adversity to learn how to deal with it.

I started to want to prove to my mother that I was worthy of her love and not just a wimp. As I was looking at my brother and sister, who were doing everything well, I was trying my best to compensate for this weakness. As a child, I was always a bit of a perfectionist. I didn't like making mistakes, and I would beat myself up emotionally whenever I did. This desire to be perfect extended to my schoolwork and my relationships. I was a straight-A student who always tried to please my teachers, and I was always worried about what other people thought of me. I was a people pleaser, always putting others' needs before my own. I just wanted to prove that I was not all bad, that I was worthy.

Who Is Predisposed to Imposter Syndrome?

Outside of our childhood experiences, I wanted to see if there was a pattern in the types of people who are affected by the syndrome. Are there common roots? Do some personality traits affect the development of the syndrome? And does it affect both genders?

What I discovered is that there are certain groups of people who are more at risk of suffering from imposter syndrome than others. This may be linked to their personality type or their lifestyle.

People at risk of developing a negative self-image include

- students who compare themselves to their peers.
- researchers and academics who compare themselves to their colleagues.
- people who are the first in their family to succeed.

Others are constantly judging these people, and they often judge themselves harshly. They may believe that it was "too easy" for them to succeed and that they will lose their success just as quickly as they achieved it. As a result, they may develop a negative self-image and have difficulty adapting to their school or university, researcher or academic environment, or career. By comparing ourselves to others, we are setting ourselves up for failure instead of using our own unique skills and experiences to succeed.

You also find that people who did not earn their success often feel that they were just lucky. For example, someone who by chance makes a discovery that leads to success may feel that they "were just lucky" and forget all the hard work before they made the "chance" discovery. Another example is someone who inherits a business, even though they may successfully manage and grow the business for years, they may feel that they "just carried on" what previous generations built without recognizing their contributions to the success. Underrepresented groups (such as women, ethnic minorities, people with disabilities, or specific religious beliefs) may feel that their achievements are "tokens" and they did not deserve their success. Children of successful parents may feel that their success is due to their parents' achievements and not their own.

As I kept digging into my research, I realized why the rate of imposter syndrome was so high: So many different beliefs can lead to it.

One way to combat the negative effects of comparing ourselves to others is by focusing on our personal growth and development. Instead of worrying about what others are doing or achieving, we can work on improving ourselves in a way that feels meaningful to us.

Does Imposter Syndrome Affect Males and Females Differently?

In the early years of research into imposter syndrome, it seemed as if women were more likely to be affected. Clance and Imes limited their studies to female participants as they believed that the syndrome affected mostly women.

In their research, Clance and Imes found that women are not as driven as men to be successful. The reasons are complex, but one of the main factors is that society did not have the same expectations of women as they do of men. This leads to successful women doubting their abilities and often contributing their success to external factors. This may be one of the reasons women are less likely to ask for a promotion or raise.

In her book *The Secret Thoughts of Successful Women*, Young (2011) explains that even during our childhood years, boys are encouraged to be proud of their achievements and to boast while girls are taught that they should be humble and not draw attention to themselves. According to Young, girls quickly learn that there are two sets of rules, one for girls and one for boys.

Girls are judged more harshly than boys, from their physical appearance to the way that they act. This leads to girls trying to be "perfect" to avoid the criticism they fear. Young further says that women in the workplace are not taken seriously on account of their gender; unless they outperform their male colleagues, they are barely noticed. This leads women to work harder than men to achieve the same outcomes, and many women start to doubt their capabilities.

Recent research disputes the fact that women are more likely to suffer from imposter syndrome and in a 2019 study, it was found that men and women were affected equally. The study did however show that there was a big difference between the confidence level experienced by the different genders suffering from imposter syndrome in the workplace; it revealed that 79% of women versus 62% of men admitted that they did not believe that they were able to do the job expected of them (*Getting to Equal*, 2019).

These findings may be because women are more likely to admit to doubting their abilities. Stereotyping in the workplace leads to men needing to look capable and in control whereas women are not expected to act the same way. This need for men to look in charge may lead to many men secretly doubting their abilities but being too scared to admit it and to seek help. Women often do not like the spotlight and are humbler in general, making it easier for them to admit needing help and to report feelings of imposter syndrome.

As gender stereotypes change with time, we may see another shift in the ways the different genders are impacted by the syndrome over the next few years.

Fueling the Syndrome

The problem with imposter syndrome is that instead of trying to eliminate it, we unconsciously fuel it. That's what I did.

Another attack led me to act in a way that would set me on a path of no return. Back then, I had no idea that this decision would have such an impact on my life. I was only six.

This memory is forever engraved in my brain. I was at

school when it happened: As I was washing my hands in the bathroom, the excruciating pain quickly invaded and surged through my body. In less than a minute, I was unable to remain standing.

As the pain grew, I made this dreadful choice: I decided to lie. I did not see any other choice as I could not risk not going home and having to endure the pain at school. At this stage, I fully understood that my symptoms were different from a stomach bug; therefore, the teacher might not believe me. So, I decided to lie and say that I had vomited, the most common symptom of what I was always diagnosed with, which would give the proof they needed to send me back home.

What I had not realized was that lying would just increase my imposter syndrome. It made me feel even more like a fraud, a sentiment that was harder to remove than to build.

These episodes took a significant toll on my self-confidence and self-esteem. I began to work even harder than the other kids; I just wanted to be perfect to compensate for this disadvantage.

The years passed, and after a few attacks, my mother realized something was wrong. She sent me to many doctors to try to figure out what I had, but nobody could find a response. I wouldn't receive a diagnosis until years later.

I want to be clear: In no way am I mad about my mother's reaction. Being a parent is one of the hardest jobs in life, in my opinion. It is difficult to find a balance between empathy and teaching your child values. I was a kid and as a parent, it can be very difficult to understand to which extent a child is overreacting. It is easy as an adult to reflect and blame our parents for their mistakes. But they are only human, and a lot of factors that are invisible to us affect the way they act. Even the most perfect parent in the most perfect world (let me know if you find this person) will make mistakes. This is basically the definition of the human experience. And I must say that if I had been in her situation, I might have reacted exactly the same way.

My mother never learned about what I had; she passed away before I was diagnosed. She was also battling with cancer for more than a decade. When cancer got her, after 11 years of hard fighting, my father who had kept quiet for years about the possibility of me having a genetic condition that was present in his family, decided it was time for me to get checked. He knew that it would have been hard for my mother to learn this type of news and that it could kill her faster, so he remained silent. I am very grateful he did, even if not knowing what I had was painful to accept for my mother.

After years of incomprehension and questions, I was 14 years old when I finally received the clarity I had been waiting for: I was formerly diagnosed with hereditary chronic pancreatitis. As strange as it sounds, I was so happy when I learned the news. Finally, I had the answer I had been looking for. It was years of questions answered in one hour. I am truly grateful that my mother never had to know what I really had. It would have devastated her to learn that I would have to live the rest of my life with this condition. But I must say that on the other hand, a small part of me wished she had known that I was not lying.

You would think that a formal diagnosis of such a condition would be enough to wipe out all my beliefs of being a fraud. You would be mistaken.

The Power of Our Subconscious Mind

Exactly the same way as you cannot realize the irrationality of your beliefs, I could not as well.

I had spent so many years telling myself that I was just making a fuss when in fact, I had nothing, that I could not remove this idea from my head. For me, it had become normal to live in dreadful pain three months a year. I kept believing that I was weaker than others and not worthy. So I developed ways to compensate. I was on a destructive mission to prove that I was enough.

By knowing my roots, you might better understand why I reacted this way in 2020. Realizing how this event impacted me was one of the first steps that led me to freedom. I quickly identified this episode in 1997 as the root cause of many of my psychological issues and behaviors. It was sitting in my head and dictating many of my actions just below my awareness level.

As I learned about the power of our subconscious mind, I started to understand why I had struggled for so long. Our subconscious is essentially a storage unit for all of our thoughts and beliefs. It accepts every-thing we experience and believes that as fact, even if it may not be true. And the extent of the damage can be big as 95% of your subconscious mind controls your life.

This means that negative experiences, such as the one I faced in 1997, can become ingrained in our subcon-scious and ultimately affect how we think and behave. To heal and move forward, it is important to identify these experiences and actively work on rewriting the beliefs that have been instilled in us.

By recognizing the power of my subconscious mind and actively working on changing my negative beliefs, I could let go of the past and live a much happier and more fulfilled life. Understand the power of your subconscious mind and actively work on rewriting any negative beliefs that may be holding you back. It could truly change your life.

But to change our beliefs, we need to be self-aware about them and that is why I have listed self-awareness as the first step. If you have opened yourself to self-aware-ness, you will be better equipped to understand which beliefs engraved in your subconscious mind are respon-sible for your imposter syndrome. But if you do not change these beliefs, you won't be able to change how you see yourself.

Changing your beliefs will not solve all the symptoms that result from imposter syndrome, but if you do change them, you will not simply be able to eradicate the symptoms. This is why it is important to work on changing them as soon as possible.

As I said before, I truly believe that we are the author of our life. This also means that the stories we tell ourselves are the ones that limit us. If you keep telling yourself that you are not worthy of love, chances are that you will not find love. I don't mean that this is true; what I am saying is that your beliefs will lead to behaviors that will support this claim.

As we saw before, our brains build schemata to help us navigate the world. If your subconscious brain develops the idea that you are not worthy of love, you will make decisions leading to events confirming this belief.

The Link Between Decision-Making and Imposter Syndrome

Daniel Kahneman received the Nobel prize following his research on decision-making. In his book, *Thinking Fast and Slow*, Kahneman (2015) reveals that the brain has two systems that it uses to make decisions: System 1 and System 2. System 1 is fast, automatic, and emotional. It's the system we use when we're thinking intuitively, without really thinking about it. System 2 is slower, more deliberative, and more logical. It's the system we use when we're trying to make a rational decision.

When it comes to imposter syndrome, System 1 is usually in charge. We often automatically believe that we're not good enough or that we don't deserve our success. This is because we do not rationalize when making these daily decisions.

That is why, if you keep your unfounded and distorted beliefs about yourself, you will never be able to change your attitude, and you will be stuck in a vicious cycle. Your behaviors will translate these beliefs into reality. The first step to getting rid of these beliefs is to be aware of them. Once you know these thoughts are not rational, you can start challenging them. When you think you're not good enough, take a deep breath and ask yourself: "Why do I believe this? What evidence do I have to support this?" When you catch yourself thinking you don't deserve your success, remind yourself of all the hard work you've put in.

I am not going to lie; I still find myself caught up in my negative beliefs. The difference is that now I am aware of them, and I quickly analyze them so I can see if they are true or completely unfounded. Why do I not just discard them? Because sometimes they might be true, and in this case, I want to be able to learn from them and change my behaviors accordingly.

Kahneman's research on decision-making can help us understand the roots of imposter syndrome and how to overcome it. When we're aware of the two systems our brain uses to make decisions, we can see that the thoughts that lead to imposter syndrome are coming from System 1. We can also start to challenge these thoughts by using System 2.

Imposter syndrome doesn't have to hold you back.

Once you're aware of it, you can start to challenge your automatic thoughts and beliefs.

Detrimental Effects of System 1 Thinking

Despite my diagnosis, the feeling of being an imposter did not disappear as I had not worked on the roots of it. My perfectionism had allowed me to succeed academically, but this feeling of being an imposter never left. In high school, the disease became more severe, and I had to miss much of school. By the last year of high school, I was more absent than in attendance. I was furious at myself, and even though my classmates and teachers were telling me how strong I was for continuing to fight to succeed, I couldn't help but think that I had nothing and that one day they would discover what a fraud I was.

I will never forget a scene that happened during my senior year. The baccalaureate, which is the national final exam in France, was coming up. To prepare us for this major exam week, the school was offering mock exams so we could practice. These were essential exams, so I always ensured to be present during these tests. However, several students in the class did not show up (no judgment here!).

During the next class, the math teacher expressed his displeasure regarding the no-show of some of the students. And he decided to make an example of me by telling the class that even though I was sick, I had made an effort to attend the exam. Some people would feel a sense of shame to be put in the spotlight like that. Others would have been happy to be rewarded after the effort. I was neither. A rush of heat spread across my body as the fear of being found out grew. I felt ashamed for making them believe that I was sick and scared of being outed as a fraud. My anxiety level was so high that it was almost uncontrollable and incomprehensible for my entourage.

During the decades that followed my diagnosis, I only went to see my gastroenterologist twice; both times were before my majority. I stopped going because I reasoned why waste the time of a doctor for such a small condition? My father, for completely other reasons, did not want me to go as he also believed that it was nothing.

We were wrong, and I paid the price for our faulty beliefs.

The Consequences of Not Changing Your Beliefs

Changing our beliefs is hard, but not changing them could lead you to unfortunate consequences. That is why I encourage you to be less stubborn than I was and hope that you act faster than I did. By the time I finally decided to change them, I was already paying the price of regrets.

January 2020

On January 23rd, my stone had been broken, my kidney was working perfectly, and the sepsis had drastically reduced; I was now ready to restart my life and put this story behind me. Back then, I had already learned with this experience the most obvious lesson: listen to your body and trust your instinct. My childhood events were at the back of my head, too far for me to learn from. I was too happy to get back to my life that trying to work on my past demons was not on my agenda. By now, you truly believe me when I say that I am a stubborn person. You might be wondering, *What more did she need?* I have the answer to that one: much more.

I was smiling in my hospital bed while waiting for my surgeon to come and bring my release papers. I had already packed and was ready to leave. I was full of energy and ready to enjoy my weekend before the start of the workweek. But before leaving, the doctor brought with him a piece of news that would force me to change forever.

The hospital had done a routine blood test while I was there. They had seen in a previous scanner that my pancreas had suffered extreme damage and therefore decided to test my blood sugar.

The levels were too high, and therefore, my doctor advised me to get screened for diabetes. I'm sure the pack of candy I had secretly eaten the night before did not help. If I had known that I would never eat candies—or anything else—without worrying about the conse-quences, I am ashamed to say I would have eaten more.

Could I have been so blind and not realized it? I knew that diabetes was a consequence of pancreatitis. My grandmother and aunt, who also live with the condition, had developed it. However, they were at least 20 years older than I was when this happened.

After everything I had been through in the past three weeks, I decided to stop living in a nutshell and followed his advice.

The days that followed were some of the most stressful in my life. As I was anxiously waiting for the results, I could not stop myself from trying to learn about this condition. Let's just say that people who advise you to never look at Google before a diagnosis are your friends.

Being diagnosed with diabetes scared the hell out of me. The idea of living for the rest of my life dependent on insulin, or any other type of medication, frightened me. I think I reached the apotheosis of fear when I had the very good idea to watch a YouTube video on how to pack for vacations as a type 1 diabetic. The woman's bed was filled with supplies, and as she was cheerfully explaining all the "to-do" to go on vacation, my face decomposed at the same rate as the never-ending list. This was only the first video of many where I became acquainted with the numerous things I would need to do if I was to become diabetic.

I was at my work desk when I saw my hospital's email. I had pressured them to receive the results before my doctor's appointment that was planned for the same day. My hands were trembling as I pressed the button to open the attachment. My eyes were blurred due to the stress, and the amount of information in the file did not make things easier. And finally, there it was, written in black on white: diabetic[1].

At that moment, I finally realized that my life would never be the same. And I was right. It was no longer a small and unfortunate lesson that the universe had taught me. It was an indelible lesson with no possibility of erasing it.

Double-Edged Sword

In the following two weeks, I learned that my pancreatitis had eaten my pancreas, and it was no longer functioning. In addition to diabetes, I was diagnosed with severe pancreatic insufficiency, meaning that I could no longer secrete the enzymes to digest proteins and fats.

For the past three years, I had not experienced any pancreatitis attacks and concluded that I had been able to kick the condition back. I was totally wrong; it was the complete opposite. The condition had, in fact, advanced to the point where my pancreas was declared dead. I had just become pain-free, that's it.

They explained that the years of pain made me resistant to it, which is why I had not been feeling anything. Now at least, we could all understand why I had never felt the kidney stones. Being pain-free might sound like a thrill: no more cramps, stabbing pain, suffering... and I was thrilled at the beginning. That was until I realized that I could easily find myself back to a similar situation due to not feeling the pain.

Having pain is a way for your body to signal that something is wrong. It is a physiological reaction that allows us to react when needed and is crucial for our survival. Don't get me wrong; I am not looking for pain in my life, but we cannot deny how useful it is.

In addition to having low self-confidence, I had also lost the confidence I had in my body to send me a signal that something was wrong. It was like my body was punishing me for ignoring it for so many years. Consequently, it would show me how my neglect affected it even more soon enough.

Self-Harm Through Self-Experiments

Instead of facing the harsh truth, I decided to go a little bit deeper into my nonsense and raise the theory that my doctors and medical tests were wrong. In the end, we are always right in our minds (or at least we think). So I decided to test my theory in an attempt to convince myself that I was not diabetic and that my pancreas was functioning like a rock star. I would do what I called "scientific experiments" on myself to try to test whether I actually had something—which, I must say, made the conditions even worse and scared my doctors. As you can see, I am the dream patient for many doctors.

To conduct my experiments, I would not take my insulin to prove to myself I was not diabetic. I would watch my curve rising on my glucometer in despair, with only imposter syndrome as my best friend. When my curve would fall into the non-diabetic line, it comforted me in my beliefs. We all know that being part of a support group within a community is a tremendous help. But when I joined the diabetic one, it only brought me shame as I felt like a fraud in the middle of people who really had something.

I did the same thing with my pancreatitis. I didn't want to believe that I was no longer digesting. I would not take my pancreatitis enzymes, and even after losing 20 pounds of pure fat in one month, it was still tough for me to believe it was true.

I was at the same stage that you must be now. I did not realize that I was fooled by my brain. I could not believe that a simple event that took place ages ago could have an impact on my life now. I was the embodiment of confirmation bias. I would only look at the pieces of evidence that supported my beliefs. I would later learn how biases can be very detrimental to our lives. In the end, our brains can trick us in many ways.

Reforming Hypotheses

Learning how to question our beliefs in all aspects of our lives is key. We might be the hero of our own stories, but even a hero makes mistakes. However, if you learn to recognize and learn from them, they become your strengths. And that's what I did. At some point, after countless struggles, I finally decided to realize that I might have been wrong all those years. I absolutely recognize that it is not an easy task to accomplish.

I might be stubborn, but after everything I had been through, I could finally see more clearly. There is a level of stubbornness where it becomes stupidity, and I was right on this edge.

Do you know the funniest part? I had been losing my sight for a few years. I was blaming it on corporate life and the hours we spend hooked on a screen. When in fact, it was the onset of diabetes. When the sepsis started, I had reached a point where I could barely see what was in front of me. I was blind from the inside out! But as I started to get back control of my blood sugar and work on changing my beliefs, I finally started to see again.

Until we learn how to break our beliefs and repro-gram our minds, we are not free. Changing our beliefs, patterns, and behaviors, even as hard as it can be, will set us on a path of recovery.

As I am now writing this book, I am grateful for everything that has happened to me. If I had not had to go through all these adversities, I would have kept living in denial and way below my potential. It was like external forces pushed me on this journey. I am not religious, but I believe something outside our control is impacting our lives. Maybe it's just my brain trying to rationalize it, who knows? But in the end, what do I care if I am wrong? It worked.

A great thing happened when I started changing my

beliefs: I was finally ready to eradicate the many symptoms hurting my daily life. Regarding imposter syndrome, I became truly aware of how its symptoms, or the defense mechanisms I built to cover my imposter, were affecting me for a long time. But as I did not yet know their roots, I could never really successfully eliminate them. No matter how much I tried, I had almost no self-confidence, no self-esteem, could not stop people pleasing, and don't even get me started on trying to stop taking things personally.

But I finally did uncover the underlying foundations, and that's where our journey continues.

---

1. I have Type 3c diabetes, also called Pancreatogenic Diabetes. Insurance companies and some health care professionals do not recognize this condition, so we are diagnosed and treated as Type 1 diabetics. The onset of Type 3c diabetes differs from Type 1 as it results not from an auto-immune disorder but when the pancreas stops producing enough insulin due to illness or damage.

PART TWO

Crack Your Mask

3.

The Infinite Quest for Perfection

"A certain type of perfection can only be realized through a limitless accumulation of the imperfect."

- Haruki Murakami

I believe that there is a real misconception around perfectionism as it can be positive and negative. On one hand, you have striving for excellence, the positive aspect of perfectionism. It is when you work toward making something better. On the other hand, you have the "cover-up perfectionism" as I like to call it. It is the bad guy as it is the type of perfectionism that you have developed to try to cover up your lack of self-esteem and feeling of imposture. You don't want to be perfect because it makes you happy; you want to be perfect so people can love you (or at least that's what you think). It is the type of perfectionism that will harm you and that is the one we need to eliminate.

Why Do We Want to Be Perfect?

I used to tell myself that my goal for perfection was solely to be a better version of myself. We love telling ourselves lies. But was it really? Or was I just trying to escape the fact that I was unhappy with who I was? That I was afraid of making mistakes and looked at perfectionism as some sort of safety net? That I wanted so much to be seen as worthy that perfection was the only way to do it?

This question haunted me. Why did I want so much to be perfect? It was not a recent pursuit. I had chased perfection since childhood. Everything needed to be perfect for me, and most importantly, I needed to be perfect. It is a stupid dream to chase. And what does it even mean? What a perfect person is for me will be quite different from your view of a perfect person. The same goes for your work and everything you do in life.

We develop perfectionism as a coping mechanism to cover up our lack of self-esteem and worthiness. By trying to be perfect in all areas of our lives, we are trying to show and scream to the world that we are worthy of something. We strive for perfection so we can get the recognition and love of others, but we do not even agree on the definition of the perfect person. Isn't it ironic?

Trying to be perfect also gives us a sense of control. And as humans, it is one of our first needs. In their book *Never Split the Difference*, Voss and Raz (2016) explain in a very simple and real way our need for control: Our brain relates the feeling of loss of control to starvation. And what do we do when we are starving and need food? We become obsessed with it. So, in a way, perfectionism is an obsession. A dangerous one.

Because when we're focused on being perfect, we're not focused on living. We're not focused on enjoying the moment, on being present. We're not focused on relationships. We're not focused on learning and growing. We're too focused on avoiding mistakes, on being flawless. And that's not living; that's surviving. Perfectionism is a form of self-imposed oppression. It's a way of putting ourselves in a box and not letting ourselves out.

What perfectionism does is take the joy out of life. It robs us of our spontaneity, our playfulness, and our creativity. It makes us anxious, stressed, and depressed. It keeps us from taking risks, trying new things, and putting ourselves out there. It's an extremely crippling way to live.

The Detrimental Effect of Social Media

So why do we do it? Why do we put ourselves through all of this pain? I think it has to do with the fact that we live in a society that values perfection. We are constantly bombarded with images of perfection. In magazines, TV, social media, and everywhere we look, there are people with perfect lives and bodies. And it's easy to compare ourselves to them and to come up short. We start to believe that in order to be happy and successful, we need to be perfect.

Are you living the life you dream about, or are you

living a life to impress other people? The need to impress others with your perfect family, your perfect holidays, and the perfect healthy meals you conjure up every evening, stems from self-doubt and low self-esteem. You need to prove to everyone (yourself included) that you are good enough and worthy.

Unfortunately, social media and all the "perfect lives" we get bombarded with every day make it difficult to admit that our lives cannot measure up, and so we also post the perfect holiday pictures, fueling someone else's insecurities in turn. I think it has to do with the fact that we live in a society that values perfection. What's even more worrying is that this quest for perfection is not just limited to our appearance. We now live in a world where we are expected to have the perfect job, relationship, and life. And if we don't have those things, we feel like failures.

In my opinion, the rise of social media has negatively impacted our mental health. The root of the goal behind social media was noble: allow us to connect with more people globally. It should have been a wonderful and positive experience. This was a great idea, especially when we know how having and belonging to a community can benefit us. And it was—until its purposes got stripped down.

Now, we have become victims of these platforms and allow them to control our lives. The dopamine rush when the notification messages arrive to show us that someone is validating our need for attention and value sends us to heaven—at least for a couple of minutes, until we need more. This addiction pushes us to pursue a quest for perfection that is unfortunately unattainable in real life.

It is like we are now living in a world where two types of humans converge: the perfect ones that we see on social media with their flawless faces, bodies, and life and the ones in real life that cannot achieve the perfection of a filter. It's easy to start feeling like you're not good enough when you're constantly being bombarded with images of perfection. If we were conscious enough of the fact that social media has been stripped of reality, everything would be fine. But that is not the case, and that is even more worrying for the generations that have been growing up with social media.

We crave so much recognition and love from our peers that if the number of likes and comments do not match our expectations, a feeling of being worthless arises as we do not receive the validation we were seeking.

We need to realize that no one's life is perfect, regardless of what they show on social media. Everyone has their own struggles and problems. And that's okay. We don't need to be perfect to be happy and successful. We just need to be ourselves.

No one can ignore social media completely, but you can learn how to deal with it healthily. To curb thoughts of low self-esteem, remember that you are not seeing someone's complete life on social media, only the perfect bits they chose to share with you. You do not see pictures or videos of celebrities or influencers when they are sick, when they fight with their partners, or when their children are naughty. You do not see them interacting with their families (except for snippets they share with you).

If we stop endorsing the culture of "perfect lives," we will remove a lot of pressure, not only from ourselves but from everyone we interact with on social media.

The Importance of Being Honest With the Reasons Behind Our Perfectionism

We need to be honest with ourselves: If we were striving for perfection in the sole interest of becoming a better version of ourselves, we would not be stopping ourselves from making mistakes. We would pursue every dream we have, even if the possibility of failure is high, as our intentions would only be to grow.

If my quest for perfection was solely based on being a better version of myself, I would not have felt the unconditional need for things to go my way or the need to control every situation. I was afraid of making mistakes, and I thought that if everything around me was perfect, I would be happy, and life would be good.

Needless to say, this is not how it works. Life will never be perfect, no matter how much we try to control it. And that is perfectly okay. What I have come to realize is that striving for perfectionism is a way of avoiding dealing with our imperfections. It is a way of running away from who we really are.

It is much easier to live in an imaginary world where everything is perfect than to deal with reality's messiness. But the truth is, we are all imperfect beings living in an imperfect world. And that is the beauty of life.

There Is No Such Thing as Perfect

And the sooner we accept that, the sooner we can start living our lives to the fullest. You cannot be perfect at everything, and truthfully, when you think about it, if you did, you would be the most hated and boring person in the world. We strive to be perfect even if we would not even enjoy being surrounded by perfect people. Think about it: Would you read a book where the character is perfect? Where they succeed at everything they do on the first attempt? No, because the story would be boring.

Perfection is the most boring thing in the world. In the end, who likes people who are perfect?

We fall in love with characters that have flaws. In fact, we fall in love with their flaws. Ask yourself: How do you feel when you see someone who gives the impression that their lives are perfect, and they have everything figured out? They make you feel uncomfortable.

Many people resent having flaws, even though our flaws make us grow. Without them, we would just be flat and dispassionate people with no prospect of growth. Your life would be one of the most boring existences on Earth. And after you truly understand that, you will most likely want to stop trying to be perfect to really focus your time on becoming a better version of yourself.

Others' acknowledgment and validation will not make you happy. You can only be happy if you are living your life authentically—mistakes and failures included.

The Roots of Our Perfectionism

So, how do we develop perfectionism? As with everything, we need to understand the roots and debunk them so we can let them go.

Many experiences might have led you to develop beliefs that pushed you to become obsessed with perfection. You might be similar to me with a mix of different ones. It does not matter. The only thing that matters is to identify them.

Perfection Is the Only Option

One of the beliefs that commonly leads to perfectionism is that a person's worth is based on what they achieve. Some parents set the standard so high for their children that only perfect grades, winning performances, and flawless recitals are good enough. Mistakes and failures are unacceptable and sometimes even punished. If you were one of these kids and grew up in this environment, you learned that mistakes and failures are not tolerated. As an adult, the pattern continues, and you develop unrealistic expectations from people around you, especially yourself.

When I worked on trying to identify the roots of my perfectionism, these beliefs of perfection as the only option were the most crystal clear ones. As an adult, I had become allergic to failure. Me, fail? Never. And if I would foresee this possibility, I would just avoid doing the thing that would put me in that position.

To understand how I came to be this way, I revisited my childhood. Growing up as the daughter of a perfectionist mother, I would constantly hear (and feel) that second place was not an option. My siblings and I needed to be first in everything we did. It meant being the first student at school and the best in whatever hobby we had. For us, it was the only option to bring happiness to my mother.

We correlated the idea that being first meant that our mother would be proud of us. So we strived for perfection, even if it meant avoiding doing things that we loved or hiding our mistakes. I wanted so much for her to be proud that I would go to great lengths to achieve this.

One day, I am embarrassed to say, that I cried in class when I received an A grade, to my classmate's greatest annoyance. Yes, I was actually this annoying kid. But my classmates did not know that I had been primed to think only A+ was acceptable. And if I did not achieve this grade, I would drag my mother's feelings down, which was one of my greatest fears. And to an extent, it was an unfounded one.

My siblings were the same. My brother quickly became an expert at hiding his test results under his bed.

Though, he was caught once, and let's just say that it taught us a great lesson. His hand must still feel the pain of writing "I should not lie to my mother" 500 times.

As I am writing these words, my mother sounds like a horrible person—the total opposite of what she actually was. I could not have dreamt of a better mother. The problem is that, as a kid, I could not understand why it was so important to her for us to be first; also, my interpretation of her expectations was distorted. Yes, she wanted us to be first, but not at the cost of our happiness and mental well-being. For example, she congratulated me when I brought back my A grade. I had spent an entire class in tears at the fear of disappointing her when I did not. It was I who had exaggerated her wish to an extent that my expectation for perfection became even higher than hers.

As an adult, I now understand how my mother came to think this way, and the motive behind her wish for perfection. The only thing she wanted the most was for us to succeed in life. She had not had an easy one, far from it, and wanted the best for us. She did not realize how this quest for perfection would lead us on a completely different path than the one she intended.

Being a parent is hard, as I said before, and most of them have only one wish: to see their kids succeed and be happy, whatever it means. But sometimes, they take the wrong approach to achieve it. We should also never forget that our parents also bring with them the scars of their past. We also need to consider the society and world in which they grew up that impacted how they think.

And there is a vicious cycle to consider: When perfectionism erupts from this type of experience, the child who grew up believing that mistakes are bad and perfection is the only way, will teach their kids the same things in return. Until someone breaks this negative pattern, it goes on from one generation to the next. So, be the one who stops it.

The ultimate issue is that the one that never fails never wins. I learned way too late, in my opinion, this lesson: When we fail, we learn, and when we learn, we do better. By always trying to seek perfection, we are avoiding trying new things or even daring to chase our dreams. I do not know which one of the two is the worst. The problem is that perfection is not the key to success. We mostly grow when we fail.

If you are a big fan of Sara Blakely, founder of Spanx, you will recall her always telling the stories of how her father asked her and her siblings every day at the dining table where they had failed during the day. I do not know a lot of parents who do that, but I find this idea genius. With as much as a simple sentence, he most likely primed his daughter to have the mindset she needed to build the empire that she has.

You will be more successful as soon as you realize the importance of failing in life. I was completely allergic to failure, and now, it has become my fuel.

When Perfectionism Is Our Way to Try to Compensate

Another belief that can lead us to chase perfection is the need to compensate for something we see as a disadvantage. According to Carl Yung (as cited in Kelland, n.d.), one of the key figures in psychology, we often develop perfectionism as a way to make up for something we see as a deficiency. In other words, we believe that if we can just be perfect, it will somehow make up for whatever it is that we feel is lacking.

Of course, this is an unrealistic and impossible goal. But that doesn't stop us from trying. We become fixated on the idea of perfection, and we'll go to great lengths to try to achieve it. Unfortunately, this usually leads to even more feelings of inadequacy because we can never quite reach that impossible standard.

That need to compensate is the root I identified most recently. When I learned about Yung's theory, it hit me like a slap in my face. Suddenly, I finally realized how much my conditions had been a driving force in my quest for perfection. I thought of sickness as a weakness; therefore, I was trying my best to be perfect everywhere else where I had more control. Not knowing what I had growing up made me see myself as a weak and less worthy kid. I was not as strong as everyone else. I could not even walk when they could play, even when they were sick.

Being perfect became a way for me to cope with this

dreadful disadvantage. But in my family, I was not the only one who felt this way. My mother, too, saw her cancer as a sign of weakness. She couldn't even bring herself to admit to the people around her that she was sick. It was a weakness, and for her, weakness was one of the worst flaws a human could have. As I grew up, I shared her beliefs. I would do my best never to let any signs of weakness show through. Even when I faced the worst news, I could only confide in Aurore and my father, the only people I trusted enough to show a glimpse of weakness.

To others, I was this superwoman who was successfully able to pull herself up despite adversity. And to some extent, I was this person, but I also consciously hid the imperfect moments. The ones where I cried in despair and regret at the thought of how hard it was to handle everything and what could happen to me next. But as perfectionism was the only way to live for me, I could not, even to my best friends, tell them my fears and worries. I could not admit my mistakes as they would make me look less perfect. I felt ashamed to be that weak, and I could only fear that others would realize I was not such a perfect person. To avoid seeing the truth, I began to want to be even more perfect. I became a prisoner of my perfection, a slave to it.

Perfectionism in Place of Love

We can also develop this need for perfection as a result of a lack of love growing up. In this case, we believe that perfection is the only way to receive love. If we can just be perfect, then maybe others will finally love us the way we want to be loved. Again, this is an unrealistic goal. No one is perfect, and no one can ever be perfect. But that doesn't stop some of us from chasing after that elusive dream.

We desperately try to compensate. We start to believe that when we are not loved, it is because of us. When in fact, some parents just lack the ability to love their children in a healthy way. No matter how much we try, we can't make them love us. So we start to believe that if we can just be perfect, they will finally see and love us the way we want to be loved. It is a destructive thought pattern that can lead to a lifetime of misery.

I was lucky to have grown up in a loving family. Not everyone has this privilege; if you did not, you need to realize that you are enough. You need to realize that you were not the problem nor at fault for this lack of love. No child deserves this treatment, and it is not your fault. You are worthy of love, and you deserve to be loved. Even if you are imperfect. But most importantly, you need to love yourself because no one can love you if you do not.

Chasing perfection does not make us better. It makes us a prisoner of ourselves. The more I lost control of the perfect life I was trying to achieve and had built in my head, the more difficult it became. I began to resent even more the weaknesses in others. How could they show their weaknesses? Why did they not want to be perfect? What I did not realize is that my resentment was, in fact, envy. I wanted to let go of this uncontrollable need. We think all we want is to be perfect when what we really want is to be free of the need to be.

So I worked harder in all areas of my life. Until I could no longer be. The cost had become so high to pay. Perfection, instead of being a strength, started to become my biggest weakness. That's when we realize this and how much we have lost that we begin to see again clearly. So how much did you lose?

The Cost of Perfectionism at Work

Only recently have I realized that my quest for perfectionism was more harmful than helpful as I would strive to control everything. One of the areas where perfectionism is the most biased is in the workplace. We value perfectionism, thinking that it will make the employee work harder. We think it is an asset for our companies when it might be quite the opposite.

It is funny as I myself was completely blind to how my perfectionism was unhealthy. I even used my quest for perfection during my job interviews as the answer to the question, "What is your biggest flaw?" I would use this as a way to make a flaw seem like a strength as I falsely believed it was actually a positive trait by saying, "I am such a perfectionist that sometimes it can be difficult for others." And the recruiters fell for it. However, they did not see the downside of perfectionism:

- micromanagement
- controlling behavior
- burnout
- lack of innovation due to the fear of failing

And I believed the same thing as them. I saw perfectionism as an asset. But if I was now in the seat of the interviewer and a candidate told me the exact same words, I would smile and give them a copy of this book. Because no, this type of perfectionism is not an asset. It is destructive and only jails us even more in our syndrome. It screams out to the world how we desperately need recognition and love. And how we let the view of others affect our self-worth. It does not only cost us a lot, but it negatively impacts our colleagues and the company we work for without either entity realizing it.

There is nothing worse for an employee than to be managed by a perfectionist. It leads to micromanagement, which then leads to loss of purpose and control for the employee, which leads to a low sense of fulfillment at work that will affect the work and development of a company. It is a domino effect that is responsible for much unhappiness and many resignations in the workplace.

When organizational psychologists say that we do not leave companies but managers, that's often the case. I also made this mistake. Before I finally let go of my quest for perfection, I was one of these managers. Since perfection can be seen as a good thing from the outside, management teams do not often take action against them, even if it is hurting the company.

The Repercussions of Micromanaging

I knew that micromanagement was truly detrimental to a team and their well-being. Thus, when I was offered support which made me manager by default, I wanted to make sure that I would not fall into that trap. But there was a problem: I still wanted everything to be perfect.

When Tifanie joined the team, I was consciously trying not to interfere too much in her jobs while maintaining the highest, almost unreachable, standard I expected. I could not admit it to her, but I falsely believed that only I could do things perfectly. So instead of micromanaging her work by checking her every step, I came up with the idea to rework her assignments as much as possible to make them resemble what I would have done and therefore meet my standards. We can all admit that in fact, I was pretty much doing a big part of her work and showcasing a total lack of delegation. It was in fact micromanaging.

My behavior led to many various issues: because we were now a two-person team, we were expected to produce more than when I was alone; therefore, I needed to work even more. But the most shameful thing for me to admit is that it also led Tifanie to lose confidence in herself and her work. My attitude made her believe she was not doing her job well. When she made a mistake, something normal as a human, I would get frustrated and ashamed as if I had done it and failed.

This is particularly dangerous as it makes us want to control even more. I was transposing my quest for perfection to Tifanie, leading her to lose even more confidence in herself and in her ability to do the job. Which she was, in fact, doing very well. As a manager, it was my responsibility to lead her to grow in her position and learn to become the best at it, and I had failed to do so.

But in addition to being detrimental to her, it was also so for the company. How could she innovate or try new things if she saw that failure could harm her career? She could not. As we, perfectionists, cannot. When we are so afraid of failing, we become allergic to trying new things, and therefore, we stay in our comfort zone where we know that it will be perfectly done. But this comfort zone is often the one where we stop learning and progressing.

Letting Someone Make Mistakes for Success

It was not until I realized the impact of my behavior that I could start changing it. Tifanie went on to find her purpose in life and as I hired a new team member, I made sure that this time I would not make the same mistakes. It was even more important this time around as my new recruit, Antoine, was only beginning his career. Therefore, I needed to make sure that he would not be traumatized or affected from the get-go by a bad manager. I won't lie: It was *not* easy. It is already difficult to control your need for perfection with people who know what they are doing thanks to their years of experience; imagine what it is like when you have a beginner standing in front of you.

But with effort and acceptance of failure being a part of growth, I allowed him to make decisions and mistakes, standing by in case he needed help. I did not correct his work as it would have prevented him from learning. I did not make weird facial expressions as I saw some of his mistakes. I just did my best at trying to help him see where he could improve. What were the results? He came up with original, new ideas; he was not scared of expressing his opinions; he became an expert at his job and most importantly, he gained confidence in himself. And I am so proud of his achievements.

Plus, we also had many laughs at the realization of some of his unconventional mistakes.

Two Sides of the Same Coin

The reason why companies lack awareness when it comes to the problem of perfectionists at work is that feeling like an imposter does not necessarily negatively impact performance. A recent study by MIT scholar, Basima Tewfik, suggests that by trying to make up for their perceived shortcomings, people with imposter syndrome work harder than their colleagues and are very good team players with strong social skills. It is as if the "imposter" believes that they need their colleagues to help keep up the pretense that they are competent, and they become very focused on nurturing good relationships with their colleagues. Tewfik warns that despite the positive impact imposter syndrome may have in the workplace, the effect on the individual who suffers from it can, however, never be positive (Tewfik, 2022, as cited in Dizikes, 2022).

The flip side of the coin is people suffering from imposter syndrome can be so unsure about their capabilities that they procrastinate. The fear of failure and not being able to complete their work to the high standard they set for themselves causes them not to start at all. They may end up drawing up (and even discussing) their plans with colleagues, but the work just doesn't get done —the so-called "analysis paralysis." This leads to conflict with managers as work is not delivered on time, which causes more thoughts of self-doubt and feeling like an imposter.

So, even if perfectionism can positively impact the workplace, it is always at the cost of your sanity. Give yourself some tough love and address it before it is too late.

The Cost in Our Relationships

Striving for control in all things is not only harmful in the workplace but also personally. It prevented me from living my life to the fullest and truly enjoying the moment. It was also holding me back from exploring new things because I was afraid that I would not be able to do them perfectly.

In the movie industry, we are used to seeing a character who strives for perfection and ends up going down a rabbit hole. It's perfectionism that is at the center of the character's development. A famous example is Bree Van de Kamp in *Desperate Housewives*. As the series progresses, we can see how her quest for perfection leads her to lose everything she cares about and, most importantly, her family. This is not just a Hollywood story. In real life, many of us play this role that causes us to ruin relationships. And it is not only about our partner or spouse; it also affects our children and friends.

By wanting to control everything in our lives so that nothing goes wrong, we end up creating the opposite. And to top it off, this need for control often leads to anxiety and stress. We can easily become overwhelmed when we constantly try to meet our own high standards. This can lead to us being critical of ourselves and others. We can also become inflexible and resistant to change. Try to realize the burden it represents for us and our entourage.

We have seen previously, as a parent, you could pay an even higher price: passing down your flaws to your offspring. Society expects us to instinctively be competent parents. The issue is that no one has the perfect instruction manual on how to be a parent. And even if such things exist, what I came to learn in life is that what is taught in a textbook does not take into consideration our environment and life events. They are perfect theories that only apply to a perfect world. Thus, most parents learn by trial and error and fall back on their own experiences with their parents (which may not have been ideal). This means that mistakes are made no matter how hard you try. But the harder you try to be perfect, the more mistakes you will make.

I have seen it firsthand: When my mother had only our best interests at heart, her blindness toward her unhealthy view of perfectionism made her achieve the complete opposite. Unfortunately, children learn what they see, and a mother's self-doubt can harm her children and lead to another generation of people feeling that they are not good enough.

Perfectionism can also lead us to withdraw from our relationships altogether for many reasons. We may stop spending time with our partners or friends because we fear that they will see our flaws. We may also stop sharing our feelings and thoughts because we fear being judged. Some parents may avoid gatherings or outings with other parents as they believe that they cannot compare and that they will be discovered to be incompetent.

The only thing we gain when we do that is to become perfect but alone. And let me tell you, that is not a good thing. According to a study done by Tiwari (2013), loneliness is as lethal as smoking 15 cigarettes per day, so beware.

Perfectionism can also damage our relationships in more subtle ways. For example, we may constantly criticize our partner's actions or words in an attempt to get them to meet our high standards. We may also have difficulty receiving compliments or praise from others because we think they must be wrong or that they don't understand the whole picture. It is important to remember that nobody is perfect and that we all make mistakes. Our relationships will be more fulfilling when we accept ourselves and others for who we are.

Ultimately, perfectionism can lead to feelings of isolation, loneliness, and disconnection in our most important relationships. It can also prevent us from forming new relationships or deepening the ones we have.

The decision is entirely up to you: Are you willing to pay this price for perfection? I knew I was not and that's why I decided to try my best to let it go.

Ending the Destructive Pattern of Perfectionism

Until 2020, my perfectionism didn't get too much in my way, or so I thought. I would strive to be the best at everything, not for myself, but for others, so they could see how worthy I was. It is tough to admit, especially in today's world, where admitting the real reason why we do things is a sign of weakness. But I decided before I wrote this book that I would be entirely honest, so I am. I did not chase perfectionism to become a better version of myself. I chased it to get recognition, support, and love from others.

Once again, I had to be pushed into the blackest hole to fix my quest for perfectionism. Do you know what can be the worst enemy of a perfectionist? For me, it became my diabetes (or at least one of them).

Let me explain to you quickly what having diabetes is. Having diabetes is like looking to your right and left before crossing the street. When you see no cars coming, you believe that it is safe to cross, so you go ahead, before being hit by a plane. This metaphor truly embodies how I came to understand what managing diabetes was: You have to do the job of an organ based on multiple factors that you have no control over.

To give you an idea, it is believed by medical research that 42 factors influence our blood sugar levels daily. These include your level of sleep, the weather, stress level, the food you eat, and when you eat it, to name a few. As you can imagine, it is not a piece of cake to try to control it externally. As a diabetic, you try your best to figure it out, but striving for a perfect non-diabetic line every day at all hours is almost impossible. I would be more confident trying to build a spaceship than promising a perfect blood sugar line all my life.

But of course, I did not think like this when it all started. I intended to be the most perfect diabetic person. I did not want to be within the recommended range for diabetics. I wanted to be in the one for non-diabetics. After all, I had always been successful at achieving what I wanted because of my perfectionism, so this was just another challenge. In addition to being stubborn, you can now see that I also was a know-it-all.

Let's just say that it taught me a great lesson. I did manage to stay in this perfect line for a few months, but it almost cost me my sanity and transformed me into an obsessive person. It was not a plane that I took in my face; it was like I had been attacked by an entire army as I tried to keep up with my new challenge.

To be able to achieve these numbers, I followed a drastic diet where all forms of carbohydrates and sugar were banned. In our modern world, this translates to spending hours in the supermarket trying to figure out what you can eat. I would not take my enzymes, so the amount of food I was digesting would be less. But even this was not enough. I had to walk after each meal to try to maintain the numbers. Don't get me wrong, I love walking, and its positive effects on health are scientifically proven (more on that in Chapter 8). The problem is when walking as soon as you finish eating becomes mandatory: This lifestyle is hard to maintain in normal social settings.

But despite all these efforts, it became increasingly harder to keep this perfect line. I sometimes walked for more than an hour in despair when I saw my numbers rising. I started to develop a fear of this sharp arrow that our glucometer displays when our blood sugar is rising fast. It soon became a nightmare. I was obsessed with my blood sugar. I would scan my continuous glucometer every 10 minutes, trying to analyze all my actions so I could understand patterns that would help me reach my goal.

I reached the point of no return when I would not even accept a dinner invitation out with friends for fear that I would not be able to walk afterward and, therefore, would not be able to have my non-diabetic golden line. When I think that I spent hours of my life trying to figure out an excuse as to why I had to leave a dinner early so I could walk, I'm glad that shame doesn't kill because I wouldn't be here anymore.

Recognizing the Benefits of Not Being Perfect

This was when I recognized that I needed to change before my perfectionism started to consume me. I needed to accept that sometimes things can be imperfect—how difficult that was.

I decided to let go of this need to always be perfect and accepted my (many) flaws instead. It was tough, I must say, especially when you have spent your life thinking that being perfect is the most important thing in the world.

The quest for perfection may, on the surface, not look like a problem. But it is when the primary motivation to be perfect is driven by self-doubt and the need to feel validated becomes an issue. When we set the bar for our quest for perfection so high that it is unachievable, it only leads us to continually feel like a failure, fueling our imposter beliefs even more. We should all strive for excellence but being a perfectionist will hold us back.

It is human to want to be loved and accepted. And I think that's what drives many of us to seek perfection. But believing that people will love and accept us if we're perfect is a false belief. And the good thing is that no one is perfect, so there is nothing wrong with being so. Seeking perfection is only going to lead to disappointment and frustration. So, if you are like me and have been chasing perfectionism, I encourage you to stop. Take a breath. And embrace your imperfections. They are what make you perfectly unique and beautifully human.

Moreover, the quest for perfection can lead you to avoid doing things you want, such as starting a new project or hobby or seeking the job of your dreams. We often see people who decide to launch businesses but end up never doing it because it is not as perfect as they want. I can definitely raise my hand as I am guilty of that one as well. Over the years, I told Aurore many times that I was starting a new business. Dozens of business plans later, one day, when I told her my new project of the moment, she turned to me and said: "It's a good idea Coline, but one day you'll have to act on it." And this time, much to her surprise, I did.

Because you know what? Life is not perfect, but that is what makes it fun.

Accepting flaws and insecurities in ourselves and others liberate us to pursue a happy, fulfilled, and meaningful life without the pressure of unreasonable expectations.

The bestselling author of *Big Magic: Creative Living Beyond Fear*, Elizabeth Gilbert (2015) believes: "Perfectionism is just fear in fancy shoes and a mink coat pretending to be elegant when it's just terrified" (p. 167). And I think she is right.

4.

Stop Taking Things Personally (It Is Not All About You)

"People tend to be generous when sharing their nonsense, fear, and ignorance. And while they seem quite eager to feed you their negativity, please remember that sometimes the diet we need to be on is a spiritual and emotional one. Be cautious with what you feed your mind and soul. Fuel yourself with positivity and let that fuel propel you into positive action."

- Steve Maraboli

As an imposter waiting to be unmasked, taking things too personally was one of my main hobbies. It is, I believe, among all the symptoms of imposter syndrome, the most common one. We are so much focused on ourselves that we forget that not everything is about us. The following story will most likely bring a smile to your face as you recognize yourself in it.

August 12th, 2022

WhatsApp to Aurore: "How are your holidays going? I see that you are having fun, I am glad you can finally enjoy some time off. On my side, I have started to sell my items. I can't wait to move to Lisbon. When will you be back?"

. . .

August 13th, 2022

7:30 a.m.

Aurore did not respond, maybe I did something wrong. Did I say something bad to someone that she could have heard? I don't recall having done anything wrong, but maybe I do not remember. Maybe it's something I did a long time ago. Come on Coline, just forget about it. She is just busy.

4:12 p.m.

She still has not responded, and it's already lunch time in France. For sure she has seen the message. I must have done something, but what is it?

August 14th, 2022

8:12 a.m.

Now I'm sure I did something wrong, my heart rate rising quickly. I just need to find out what it is and apologize. What can I do for her to forgive me?

5:14 p.m.

She is never going to talk to me again. How am I going to live without her? She is so important to me and because of a stupid thing I did, I have lost her, I am sure.

August 15th, 2022

WhatsApp from Aurore: "Hi Coline! I am sorry I only respond now, we were on a boat trip so the connection was not good."

A feeling of relief came over me as I smiled, looking at my screen. And quickly, my joy gave way to embarrassment. In what world do you put yourself through so much torment for something you are known to be an expert at?

Because yes, at this, I can confidently and without any doubts say that I am an expert at responding to messages days (and even weeks) after I receive them. I have nothing against the person, even quite the opposite. But as I open the message, I smile while reading it and think about what I will answer before putting down my phone, thinking, *I will respond later.* But guess what? I usually don't.

And even when I know that it is a common behavior among all of us (I truly admire you if you do not do that), I still believe when someone does it to me that I did something wrong. When I do not receive a quick response, a very well-developed movie will start in my head. It usually starts by trying to remember if I did something wrong (that's the moment when you find yourself regretting any type of gossip you have done), could they know about it, or maybe it's something I said the last time I saw them. Maybe they just don't like me, and they have been faking it for the past few years. In the end, why would they even like me? I am not the best at maintaining friends.

We Naturally Put Ourselves Through Hell

And here is the beginning of the torment: Your brain starts to build its own story solely based on your perception and fear, leading you to start to have a physiological response to your reaction. Anxiety and stress kick in which makes your heart rate rise and your breathing become faster; you might even get a headache or an upset stomach. You are now in a state of alertness for no valid reason at all.

In her book *Mind Over Medicine*, Rankin (2015) explains in an easy-to-understand manner how small stressors, such as taking things personally, can activate our flight or fight response. When this happens, our body releases cortisol and other stress hormones that can ultimately lead to health issues if constantly activated. The fight or flight response is a primitive mechanism that helped our ancestors survive in dangerous situations. This mechanism allowed them to fight off the threat or flee to safety when danger arose. However, in modern society, we often face constant stress and triggers that activate this response, leading to chronic activation and negative health effects.

I used the message example as it is by far the most common event where we mistakenly believe that something is because of us when it is not. And it is quite funny as we are in turn doing it ourselves to others. So we are mutually putting ourselves through hell.

We usually understand that we are irrational, and our fears are most likely false, but we still get caught up in our stories. However, the majority of the time, we are wrong when we think that someone is talking about us, but it does not stop us from believing it.

This example is only one of many. Below are some other common scenarios:

- If someone is acting distant, we start to think that it is because we did something wrong when in fact, this person might be going through a rough patch.
- We mistakenly believe that our boss is talking about us when they are not.
- If someone responds to us in a harsh tone, we automatically start thinking that it is because we have done something wrong when in reality, they probably have a totally other reason, such as a bad night's sleep.

We all have good and bad days. And sometimes, when it's not a particularly good one, we have the tendency to be harder on the people around us. That does not mean that they have done something wrong. And when we react this way, it is because of how we feel, not how they acted.

But in the end, taking things personally has more to do with how we see the world rather than how the world really is. Once again, it is our perception of the situation that leads us to take things personally more than the actual situation itself.

We all have this one thing about us that is just plain weird. When we get mad, it's usually not at someone else but instead, against ourselves and what could've been done differently in order to avoid feeling so terrible afterward! Indeed, in his book *The Power of Now,* Tolle (2004) talks about how when we get angry, it is not the other person that we are really mad at, but rather a projection of our own inner anger.

For example, if someone cuts us off in traffic, we might get angry and think that they are a terrible driver. But the reality is that we are just projecting our own anger and frustration onto them. The truth is, we don't really know why they cut us off. Maybe they were in a hurry, or maybe they didn't see us. But either way, getting angry at them is not going to help the situation.

The same thing goes for when people say hurtful things to us. It is easy to take those things personally and think that they are saying them because they hate us or because they want to hurt us. But the reality is, most people are just projecting their own inner pain onto us. When someone says something mean to us, it is more about them than it is about us.

So why do we always think that everything revolves around us? Why do we believe people are always talking about or trying to hurt us? The answer might lie in our ego. Our ego is what tells us that we are the center of the universe and that everything revolves around us. It's what makes us feel special and unique, and it's also what makes us susceptible to taking things personally.

But let me tell you something: If we are all the heroes of our own stories, this means that everyone is a hero and that, in fact, nobody really pays attention to what we do.

See, the great thing about that is you can stop being afraid of what people will think when you try something bold and new, as everyone is too focused on themselves to scrutinize your move.

Taking things personally can have a negative impact on our mental and physical health as we have seen. But before we can change it, let's understand all the reasons why we take things so personally.

Why Do We Take Things Personally?

We know how taking things personally affects us in a negative way. We know it is a bad habit, but it seems complicated to resist the thoughts that come to our minds.

I was fully aware of this flaw and how it affected me. But I could never resist the urge to think that I had done something terrible when someone would not respond or talk to me harshly or provide justification for things that were out of my control. It became complicated for me to manage at work as my position often exposed me to these situations. I was the person in charge of presenting work I did not do, and even if it was not my work that was judged, I was the one receiving the feedback. And when that feedback was negative, I would start to indulge in a monologue trying to justify something that had nothing to do with my work.

I would then think about the event for hours and sometimes days. The physiological response that these unnecessary stressors caused started to worry me. As a diabetic, I could no longer ignore my blood sugar rising as my fight and flight response activated. The numbers were there to prove its detrimental effect on my body, and my health was now my priority.

That is how I started my journey of trying to find the roots of why we take things personally. And I realized that many reasons lead us to behave this way, which might explain the high prevalence of this symptom in humans.

Our Fundamental Need to Belong

One theory that could explain our behavior is that we have a fundamental need for love and approval; when we don't get it, we feel rejected. According to DeWall, "Humans have a fundamental need to belong" (as cited in Weir, 2012, para. 5). We thrive in community, and the idea of being rejected by it puts us in the darkness of hell.

When we experience rejection, it activates the same pain pathways in our brain as when we feel physical pain. This is why rejection can feel so excruciating and overwhelming.

When someone does not respond to us, we fear being rejected and anticipate the feelings even before knowing whether it is true or not.

Sometimes, you will even fear rejection from someone you just met even if you do not yet know if you also like them. It is like we are pushed to seek validation and acceptance from others without questioning our feelings about them. We constantly seek love and approval from others, but what we really need to do is to learn to love ourselves first. Only then can we truly accept the love and acceptance of others without feeling the fear of rejection.

Being rejected is part of life. We will never be able to be loved by or please everyone. It is crucial to understand this, as failing to do so will lead us to worsen the view we have of ourselves. And we should never forget to ask ourselves, do we like everyone we meet? Most probably not.

We should also remember that rejection does not define who we are as a person. It may hurt, I do not deny it, but we cannot allow the point of view of others to constantly affect us as a person. So next time you fear rejection, remember that your need for love and approval should come from within yourself before seeking it from others.

But why do we crave love and approval so much? Evolutionary psychologists believe that our ancestors who had strong social bonds with their communities were more likely to survive and pass on their genes. So, this need to belong could be hardwired in us.

Additionally, Baumeister et al. (2005) explains that being rejected or excluded by a group can severely affect our self-esteem and self-worth. We may even become isolated, and isolated individuals are at higher risk of depression and anxiety disorders.

Although the fear of rejection can sometimes lead us to conform to societal norms or give in to peer pressure, it is also important to remember that we deserve love and acceptance for who we indeed are. We must surround ourselves with a supportive community that understands and accepts us. And if we encounter rejection, we must remind ourselves of our self-worth and continue pushing forward in the search for belonging.

How Our Brain Is Wired

Have you ever noticed that people will often pay more attention to the negative details when something terrible happens than they do to what was happening before? What's the importance of being told something positive versus negative? Our brains pay more attention to bad news than good!

I'm sure you've heard this one before, but it's true. According to studies in neuroscience, our brain pays close attention and absorbs negative information much better than positive details.

This may be because our human brain is explicitly wired for negativity. This is called the negativity bias, a survival mechanism that helped our ancestors avoid danger.

However, in today's modern society, where physical threats are less common (the chances of being chased by a lion are slim, we can assume), this negativity bias can lead to excessive worrying and negative thinking patterns. In his book, *How to Stop Worrying and Start Living*, Carnegie (1998) explains how worry can often be about things that haven't even happened yet. We ruminate on possibilities, creating worst-case scenarios in our minds and ultimately negatively impacting our well-being. Understanding this biological tendency can help us become more aware of our thought patterns and work toward reframing them into a more positive mindset.

In addition to the negativity bias, our brain also tends to dwell on thoughts and emotions associated with past events or future worries. This is known as rumination and can contribute to anxiety and depression.

So how do we combat this natural inclination toward negativity and worry? Carnegie suggests practicing mindfulness and living in the present moment as one way to manage worry. Challenging negative thoughts and reframing them into more positive or realistic perspectives can also help manage anxiety.

Worrying about things that haven't happened yet can be a common and natural human tendency, but it doesn't have to consume us. By understanding the negativity bias and finding ways to manage worry, we can learn how to live in balance with these thoughts.

Self-Doubt

We often project our insecurities and doubts onto other people. We think people doubt our abilities when in reality, we are the ones doubting. We attach meaning to what others say or how they act based on our beliefs. If we believe we are in a position at work that we do not deserve and expect to be found out as an imposter, we will inter-pret our colleagues' feedback through that filter. We will perceive judgment where it was not meant; we will only be able to see what we expect and dismiss the rest.

Because I doubted my ability to do the work, I was always on the defensive. And even when we receive compliments and accolades from others, we brush them off as we do not believe we deserve them, but the criticism will sting even if it was not meant to.

This need to believe that the universe revolves around us seems arrogant until we scratch a little deeper to find the real culprits—self-doubt, imposter thoughts, and the need for constant validation that we are good enough. We take things personally because, on some level, we do not feel good enough. We seek validation from others because we cannot give it to ourselves.

The solution is to pause and question the thoughts that come up. Are they based in reality or does insecurity fuel them? It takes practice, but with time, we can learn to give ourselves love and validation instead of constantly seeking it from others. This will allow us to respond calmly and rationally to situations instead of letting our self-doubt cloud our perception.

It will also allow us to have more meaningful relation-ships as we will not take things personally and, instead, focus on the real issue at hand. Imagine how annoying it is for our entourage. Do you want to spend your time constantly reassuring someone? No. You will do it for a bit, but after repeating the same thing a hundred times, you will most likely get annoyed and start to believe that, in fact, this person is right.

How to Stop Taking Things Personally

To get rid of this habit, we will again need to put in some effort. At least in the beginning. Once we have done the process a couple of times, we will have rewired our brain, making us forget our past endeavors.

There is no magic pill to stop taking everything personally: We need to change the way we think when these situations erupt in our life. That's what I did, even if it was very uncomfortable for me to do so. Remember, our brain does not like it when we try to change ingrained patterns or behaviors. It may resist and even try to pull us back into old habits. However, we can rewire our brains by creating new neural pathways with persistence and determination.

Take Control of the Voice Inside Your Head

Understanding some basics about brain biology is essential to understand the process of rewiring. Our brains are made up of billions of neurons that communicate through electrical and chemical signals. These connections between neurons are called neural pathways and can be strengthened or weakened depending on our actions and behaviors.

The associated neural pathway becomes stronger

when we repeatedly engage in a specific behavior. That's how you built the strong habit of taking things personally. This is also why habits can be so difficult to break—the neural pathway has been reinforced over time. However, by consciously attempting to change our behavior, we can also strengthen new neural pathways and overwrite old habits.

I guess you understand where I am going: To stop taking things personally, we need to change our thoughts and reactions when facing the situation. Let's look at an example: You are waiting for your friend to respond to a dinner invitation you sent the day before. Instead of starting your detrimental movie running in a loop in your head, admit your irrationality out loud. Tell the voice inside your head that it is false. Remember all the times you faced this situation and were wrong. If talking does not work, write it down. Writing has extraordinary powers that we tend to forget. It allows us to see the truth more clearly and calm our minds.

Take Control of Your Emotions

Don't deny the emotions you feel—they do exist; repressed emotions are never a solution. Instead, label them. In psychology, it is called affect labeling, and studies have shown its strong impact in reducing negative emotions. In a study by Lieberman et al. (2007), they found that labeling emotions activated the prefrontal cortex and decreased activity in the amygdala, which is responsible for fear and anxiety.

The prefrontal cortex is the region of your brain responsible for rational thought and decision-making, while the amygdala is known for its role in emotion processing. They concluded that affect labeling improves emotional regulation and decreases stress levels. This can positively impact your overall emotional well-being and can even strengthen connections in the brain.

Furthermore, labeling emotions has been shown to improve problem-solving skills and increase self-awareness. By labeling our feelings, we acknowledge that they are accurate and valid, allowing us to understand and manage them better. The more we do this exercise, the more impact it will have over time and help diffuse negativity. Like everything in life, becoming an expert at something takes practice.

When I first started doing affect labeling, I was terrible. I could not even find the words to define why I was feeling a certain way. But even with how uncomfortable it was, I kept trying to write in my journal (my favorite way to process my thoughts), and slowly I became better at it. It became easier for me to recognize the roots and the motives behind my emotions.

This powerful practice allows us to better understand ourselves and our reactions to certain situations. It helped me understand emotions in other areas of my life. So don't push aside or ignore your feelings. Instead, the next time you feel overwhelmed with them, take a step back, label them, and allow your brain to process them effectively.

Once you have changed your thoughts, change your actions. Instead of waiting by the phone, go for a walk or call someone else to distract yourself from obsessing over when or if they will respond. This is just one example, but by consistently challenging your thoughts and behaviors, you can rewire your brain and stop taking things personally.

Embrace Criticism

Learning how to stop taking things personally also means learning how to take criticism. One of the biggest hurdles in learning to take criticism well is letting go of the feeling that it is a personal attack. It can be difficult not to internalize negative feedback, but it's important to remember that criticism is intended to help us improve and grow. Instead of viewing criticism as an attack on our worth or character, we must try to reframe it as constructive feedback on our actions or behavior.

This shift in mindset can help alleviate the initial hurt or defensiveness, allowing us to assess and consider the criticism being given objectively. It's also helpful to remember that everyone has room for improvement and receiving criticism does not make you inferior or inadequate.

Additionally, try to focus on the specific points being raised rather than getting caught up in your emotions.

This allows you to address the issues at hand and work toward improvement without getting distracted by hurt feelings.

Taking constructive criticism is very important as it can help us move forward and grow. However, it would be best if we also recognized when criticism is not intended for us and, in fact, a defense mechanism by the criticizer (as discussed in the beginning of this chapter). This can be particularly hard to let go of as we see it as unfair. But there is nothing we can do about it as only the criticizer can work on their self-awareness. I am always amazed by the amount of hate comments that an article describing the success story of someone can bring. But when you dig deeper, you realize that it is often not about the subject but instead reflects the failure or jealousy of the haters.

Instead of letting this type of criticism bring us down, we should use it as an opportunity to reflect on our own actions and intentions. Are we genuinely trying to work toward our goals and staying true to ourselves? Are we surrounding ourselves with positive influences who will lift us up rather than bring us down? Let's surround ourselves with positivity and continue to work toward our goals.

Remember, it is not worth expending energy on those not genuinely trying to help or improve us. Focus on yourself and let go of any negative criticism that does not serve a purpose in your growth and development. It may not be easy, but ultimately it is the best thing for you and your future. Keep pushing forward and let go of any negativity that may hold you back.

The Power of Actions

During one of my psychology classes, we had to watch and discuss a very interesting TedTalk on how not to take things personally. It's an exciting technique that seemed original but clever at the same time, so I had to share it with you!

In this video, Imbo (2020) tells the story of how he used to take everything personally and let the opinions of others shape his self-worth. To fix this habit, he decided to become a football referee and exposed himself to constant criticism. By facing this criticism and realizing it was not personal, just a response to his actions, he learned how to stop taking things personally in all aspects of his life.

This technique may seem extreme, but it can also be applied in minor ways. Next time someone critiques or criticizes you, take a step back and analyze the motive behind their criticism. Is it because they genuinely want to help you improve, or are they just trying to tear you down? Recognizing the difference can allow you to separate yourself from the criticism and not let it affect your self-worth.

Of course, there will always be times when we take things personally and let these feelings get to us. We are only human. But by actively exposing ourselves to criticism and analyzing its motive, we can learn how to stop taking things personally and focus on bettering ourselves instead.

It's important to note that our brains constantly change and adapt, even as we age. So don't take your 20-plus years of experience in taking things personally as an excuse not to act differently.

How You Talk to Yourself Matters

Self-talk is the ongoing internal dialogue we have with ourselves. It is the voice that tells us: "It is not even worth trying, you cannot succeed" or "Give it your best shot. Even if you don't succeed, you will learn something new." And guess what? We are in control of that voice!

The way we talk to ourselves matters as it also affects how we feel about ourselves. In fact, our brains believe what we tell it. If we constantly have negative self-talk, our brains will start to believe those negative thoughts and affect our actions and emotions in a negative way. But if we consciously focus on having positive self-talk, our brains will begin to believe those positive thoughts and ultimately lead to more positive emotions and actions. If you keep telling yourself negative things, you will continue feeling bad about yourself.

Self-talk is such a critical part of psychology and many studies have been conducted to investigate this practice. A 2014 study found that people talking about themselves in the third person tend to have more positive internal conversations than those who use the first person.

According to the study, it is better to tell ourselves, "She deserves this promotion," rather than, "I deserve the promotion." I know it sounds strange, but at this point, trying will only be positive (Kross et al., 2014).

And if we have a negative reflection of ourselves, we will be more inclined to take everything people tell us personally. We will not be able to distinguish when they are only projecting onto us something that troubles them. We will automatically believe that they are right. That is why it is important to be aware of our self-talk. Consider if you would speak this negatively to someone else. Most of the time, you probably wouldn't, so apply this concept to yourself.

I used to be so skeptical about this concept. How could I, by only talking, influence how my brain thinks? Let's just say that now, I never believe every stupid thing I think. We need to learn how to control our thoughts so we can live better.

The good news is that we can practice and learn to change our self-talk. In addition to speaking nicely to ourselves, we should understand how we can be prone to overthinking.

Overthinking is the source of many critical thoughts; replaying scenarios in our head and imagining what we should have done or said differently causes a small mistake to snowball into a disaster in our mind. An example of this is when we have made an uninformed remark in a meeting and were corrected by our colleagues. We think about how stupid we were all day, lay awake at night, and the next morning, gather the courage to apologize (once again) to our manager for our stupidity.

To our astonishment, most of the time, the person doesn't even remember our remark, something that in our head snowballed into a huge mistake. But it was so unimportant to other people that they don't even remember it. How ironic life can be sometimes!

In a 2020 interview with Tim Ferriss, well-known motivational speaker Brené Brown called the negative voice in her head a "gremlin." By giving the voice an identity, she distances herself from it and can objectively look at her self-talk to change it. This is something we can try; I will call mine a "troll." What about you?

5.

Build Ultimate Confidence

"Because one believes in oneself, one doesnt try to convince others. Because one is content with oneself, one doesnt need others approval. Because one accepts oneself, the whole world accepts him or her."

- Lao Tzu

I mposter syndrome is characterized by thoughts such as "I am not worthy" or "I don't deserve this." These thoughts originate from low self-esteem that then leads to a lack of confidence. So you guessed it: Until we fix our low self-esteem, our chances of feeling confident about ourselves are slim.

The Role of Low Self-Esteem in Imposter Syndrome

To understand how low self-esteem can lead to imposter syndrome, we need to understand the difference between self-esteem and self-confidence. Self-confidence is the belief that you can do something, whereas self-esteem is an ingrained belief about who you are. If you have low self-esteem, by default, you will have low self-confidence. If we excel despite low self-confidence (in other words, we do not think we're capable of the achievement), we feel as if we do not deserve the achievement and worry others may find out that we are incompetent; the achievement was "lucky." The imposter in our mind is created.

Building ultimate confidence might be one of the biggest challenges for an imposter. At least, it was for me. But the efforts you will put toward this step are crucial when you know how confidence plays a role in your life.

To build confidence in ourselves, we must erase self-doubt and build self-esteem as all these emotions intertwine. If we doubt our abilities, we will never be able to have good self-esteem. And if we have low self-esteem, how can we feel self-confident? We just cannot. And that is why we need to rewire our brain and one by one debunk the beliefs that led us to low self-esteem so we can finally build confidence in ourselves.

I had very low self-esteem until recently. I was, however, an outstanding actor and able to hide it quite well from people around me. I would demonstrate confidence at work and in my personal life. However, deep down, my behaviors clearly showed quite the opposite when you analyzed them. They revealed how I doubted my abilities.

My salary was the most prominent result of my low self-esteem and self-doubt as an adult. I could never honestly negotiate it as I doubted my ability to do my job too much. And my fear of not being up to the task was too high for me to act. So I stayed frustrated for years, working harder and harder, trying to prove my worth, wrongly thinking that if I deserved it, they would give it to me.

The problem is that if you doubt your abilities, you cannot expect people to see you as valuable. That's particularly the case in the workspace. Even if they see you as valuable, why give someone something they don't ask for? Some companies do, but they are in the rare part of the spectrum. So you get caught in a situation where your fears stop you from asking something while rumination and frustration slowly build as you see others obtaining what they want.

I got caught up in this vicious cycle. The low self-esteem that I had developed as a kid due to my disease and abandonment was now affecting all areas of my life. I was completely aware of my low self-confidence for years (one of the rare things I was aware of), and I tried fixing it by following methods by well-known therapists and psychologists. I kept repeating affirmations in front of my mirror, "I am enough," writing them down every morning, and so on. They did work to some extent. As seen in the previous chapter, what we say to our brains has a powerful effect. But it was only on the surface. And there is an apparent reason why they could not work as much as I was trying to convince myself that I was a worthy and confident person: I did not believe it.

It was only when I changed my perception of my condition, the root of my low self-esteem, that I began to change. As ironic as it may sound, it was the last consequences of my disease that finally helped me open my eyes to my abilities. Little did I know that it would be the one that would transform me the most, eliminating my doubts, and finally giving me self-confidence.

I realized the true meaning of the concept and through adversity, we grow the most. Despite all the challenges, I still lacked confidence in myself. I would need to undergo one more surgery, the hardest of all, to finally learn the lesson the universe was trying to make sure I understood. The universe went hard on this one, but ultimately, I am grateful.

The Cost of Low Confidence

My lack of confidence in myself affected not only my work but my personal life as well. Do you remember when I mentioned at the beginning of the book that many times during my journey I thought I had finally got rid of my demons when it was only on the surface? My lack of patience had made me desperately want to believe that I was finally free from the symptoms of imposter syndrome before it was genuinely the case. I was finally able to repair deeper issues, and I did so with confidence.

Why did I desperately want to erase this feeling of low confidence? Because I realized how much it affected my life and well-being and was pissed at myself for not acting on it. I could see the businesses I could not build anymore because I did not trust myself. I saw the relationships I ran from because I could not believe someone would want to be with a sick person. I saw the work opportunities I was missing because I was too scared of failing and didn't think myself capable of succeeding in them.

So, I bought the book I thought would make me become confident as fast as it would take me to read it. Marisa Peer needs no introduction; she is a widely recognized therapist specializing in the realm of confidence. Peer is top-notch in her field, and I am grateful for the value she brings to the world. I am not saying her book was not helpful, but even the best cannot help those who do not wish to be honest with themselves. I finished Peer's book *Ultimate Confidence* and duly completed the exercises that would lead me to become the nondestructive, confident person I wanted to be.

I forced myself to believe that "I was enough." And falsely thought that it would be easy enough, right? Maybe too easy. But I did not want to look inside myself to see how I truly felt and just decided that I was now confident.

Detrimental Compartmentalizing

Therefore, I decided it was time to start dating again, as I was confident enough to do so. I took new photos for my dating profiles and was ready to play the game of modern dating (this subject also deserves a book on its own if you ask me). But there was one problem: I was fooling myself with my "so-called" confidence. However, my behaviors were the complete opposite of a confident person.

I had this terrible belief that if I wanted to meet someone, I needed to hide the fact that I had chronic conditions. I truly believed that it was a real disadvantage in dating (and life) and that no one would want to be with a sick person. So I decided to stop wearing my continuous glucometer so my condition would not show on the outside. If someone invited me to dinner (my worst fear), I would either say that I was not hungry or just eat without taking my insulin.

I was crippled with fear of someone realizing that I was living with chronic conditions. My attitude was problematic for many reasons. First, I was lying to the person, but I did not think I should have to reveal this when we first started chatting or talking. Imagine how it would sound if the first thing I said was that my pancreas is dead! I would not be surprised and would understand if the person ran away—I might have as well. But not using insulin when needed for survival shows that I didn't accept my condition. And if the relationship progressed further, they would either find out, or I would be dead by not treating my blood sugar. So, between the two, I would rather choose the first option.

Second, I told myself there were disadvantages by hiding these facts about myself. In my mind, nobody would accept being with someone like me. I completely ignored all the other parts of my personality and what I could bring to the relationship. And that's the cost of low confidence.

We are so focused on what we are not that we are completely blind to everything we are capable of doing.

But staying in this mindset, we cut ourselves off from so many opportunities that life brings. Low self-confidence can cost us relationships, careers, and even our own happiness.

When we lack confidence in ourselves, we tend to second-guess every decision we make. This hesitation prevents us from taking risks and pursuing what we truly want. In relationships, low self-confidence can cause us to doubt our worth and push away potential partners constantly. In the workplace, it can limit our potential for promotions and advancement.

Having low confidence is particularly detrimental when you face abusive individuals. These abusers prey on your self-doubt and use it to manipulate and control you. They may gaslight or invalidate your thoughts and feelings, making you second-guess yourself and believe their abusive behavior is justified. In addition, low self-confidence can prevent you from seeking help or leaving the abusive situation altogether.

We Prevent Ourselves From Realizing True Happiness

But perhaps the greatest cost of low self-confidence is missing out on the chance to be truly happy. When we constantly put ourselves down, we miss out on celebrating our own successes and learning from our failures. We sell ourselves short and hinder our own growth.

So that's why we need to shift our mindset. We need

to change how we see ourselves. I no longer see my conditions as a disadvantage in a relationship. Quite the opposite even. They show how strong I am. Thus, I no longer feel the need to hide them, nor do I proclaim them as soon as I start to speak with someone. They are just a part of who I am, and if someone has a problem with that, they have no place in my life, which is okay.

Like me, imagine everything you've lost or stand to lose due to your lack of confidence. You may hesitate to speak up in meetings, network with new people, and take on new challenges at work. Your relationships suffer because you don't believe in yourself enough to assert your needs and wants. You miss out on opportunities for growth and advancement because you doubt your abilities. So let's stop adding to the list and change instead.

Understanding Your Low Self-Esteem

There are some scenes that we live through that stay forever engraved on our mind. The one I'm about to describe was one of them. It is the moment where I honestly asked myself, "How the heck did I end up in this situation?" When I now think about it, I laugh (perhaps a little sardonically) at how life can come back to catch you when you refuse to see the reality of things.

I need to provide a disclaimer: The scene I am about to describe is graphic. I hesitated to write it but decided to go through with it as it demonstrates how we can let ourselves get very low, keeping our eyes closed to reality, and how this behavior and subsequent syndrome can be so incredibly detrimental. My case might be extreme, as you will see. But in the end, you are indulging in the same thought patterns that can lead to similar consequences.

April 2020

I was now 30 years old and desperately trying to find solutions to my newly acquired chronic conditions. In addition to all the conditions discussed previously, one last problem had come my way a few weeks before. I like to call it the icing on the cake! Almost dying from sepsis while realizing I had a blocked kidney for years and having one of my organs reject me was not enough. The universe wanted to teach me the lesson of my life. And I must say that it succeeded!

I had neglected my body for so many years, completely denying the seriousness of pancreatitis.

It was like my brain could not lie to itself anymore as it finally understood the extent of the condition. This experience taught me how powerful our brains are. You can push yourself through a lot, but it becomes hard to manage when everything comes back as a boomerang to catch you.

Only a few days after learning that my pancreas was dead, it was my rectum's turn to drop (literally). I know— I have a very glamorous life. I had been living so long with malabsorption that I had developed a rectal prolapse as a consequence. From one day to the next, I had to manage hours in the restroom with my entire rectum coming out of my body (I warned you about the graphicness). Add to that incontinence that comes with the condition; let's just say that life became exceedingly hard. And when I found myself in the bathroom with my rectum out in pain while eating candies trying to manage low blood sugar, I asked myself how I could have let myself go down this way?

June 2021

By living in denial for years, I was now paying the price. By not wanting to accept the fact that I was sick, I got even sicker. I was the sole responsible party for my adversity. And now I needed to manage all my newly found conditions while fighting my brain, which kept telling me this was nothing.

And yes, for a year and a half, I managed to convince myself that having my rectum out for up to three hours a day was not such a big deal. Something that would cost me a lot, I came to learn later on.

But I must say that I did an excellent job of trying to ignore this issue until it became no longer possible to manage. This is where you, again, must think I'm crazy, but you see, beliefs are hard to change. Look at you; how many years have you been living in disbelief? And even when people tell you that you are wrong, you still do not trust their opinion. I was the same; even with how extreme the situation was, I was fighting against beliefs that had been rooted in me all my life.

Dealing with this issue was not on my 2020 calendar. In my opinion, I had already topped off my hospital membership card by becoming a loyal customer trying to resolve my kidney and diabetes issues. And 2021 sounded way better in my mind. So, I waited to get a consultation. As time passed, I became accustomed to the situation, which had become routine. When you get used to something, it diminishes the issue.

I finally underwent my first surgery to resolve the problem. I had started the process a few months back but waited patiently to have a slot; to me, it was not such a big deal. The doctor had recommended I move on with laser surgery as it had a lower complication rate, and I would only need to stay in bed for two weeks. I would be able to resume my life within a short month and forget about these last 16 months of daily nightmares. I was ready to close this chapter of my life. I had gone through enough and believed I had learned my lessons.

However, things did not go exactly as planned. As I had let the issue go on for so long, it had reached a stage that even doctors did not anticipate. Even if they had seen that I was in the last progressive stage known for the condition, the MRI could not show the extent of the problem. Because I felt like an imposter in my situation, I was not complaining and even agreed to postpone the surgery at one point to accommodate the surgeon's busy schedule.

When I woke up from my surgery, I faced my surgeon, who was mesmerized by the situation. How could I have lived like this for so long? She had never seen the problem exacerbated to that extent before, and as patients usually overestimate their problems, she did not expect me to do the opposite. Unfortunately, the type of surgery I had couldn't completely address that magnitude of a problem. Two weeks after the surgery, the one thing I was the most scared about happened: The prolapse came back. Within weeks, it had reached the same level as before the surgery. I was at seven surgeries at that stage and would prepare for my very last.

At that moment, I understood that I would have to change my behavior and not diminish the issue anymore. I had to wait until summer passed to go back and fight for my case. There was no more only smiling and laughing in the doctor's office. I could not keep living like that. I finally understood that I needed to realize that what I was experiencing was not such a small thing and made it clear to my medical team.

So I faced the dreadful news and accepted the price of my foolishness. Because of my imposter syndrome, I encountered one last nonnegotiable fee: my ability to have children. Indeed, only one surgery was still possible, but it would cause me never to be able to have children. I accepted on the spot. I just wanted to be able to resume my life, and I was paying the price for my past mistakes. I could have avoided this situation if I had not felt like an imposter all that time. But it was too late, and the best outcome was to look positively at the problem, realizing that at least I had a solution. But most importantly, I realized I had to work on my self-doubt to avoid putting myself in a similar situation later.

That operation would be the hardest of all: hours in the operating room, having my abdomen opened, four weeks in bed without being able to carry anything, and managing work at the busiest time of the year as my unwillingness to show any signs of weakness pushed me to manage everything alone. The option of asking someone for help was still impossible for me. So I slept with the curtains open when I could not stand and transformed my bed into my house and office.

Trying to manage my recovery while continually working—from my bed—as if nothing happened, would be the most challenging but also the most life-saving experience.

After my successful surgery and resting for four days, I resumed working even if I could still not sit up. I had received time off but taking those weeks was not an option. It was the busiest period of the year at work, and nobody could back me up. I was now paying for my years of overworking, trying to compensate for my imposter syndrome. I had been able to manage a high workload; therefore, the support that I needed was not a priority for my company. I cannot blame them; every time I was given more work, I worked even harder to prove my abilities. I was also a big people pleaser, the symptom we will cover in the next chapter. So every time someone needed help, I could never conceive the possibility of saying "no."

So, when I found myself having to work 12-plus

hours a day while trying to get better, I came across a feeling that I was unfamiliar with: depression. The strength and mental energy it took me to face everything sent me to a depressive state, a feeling I had never encountered in my life, thanks to my naturally optimistic and joyful personality. On one side, my brain was telling me that I needed to push to prove my worthiness; on the other, I was starting to realize how stupid the situation was.

I had gone through many challenges and adversity in my life, but none of them had made me feel depressed, and there I was, crying alone because of my work. I was not crying because of the amount of work I had, as it typically fueled me with energy. I was crying from years of frustration that I had inflicted on myself. Years of desperately trying to prove my abilities in the wrong way.

How could I have reached a point where I would rather lie in a hospital bed than keep working? I knew working was not the issue as I was passionate about it. So what was the reason? I would find out soon enough. Suddenly, all the pieces of the puzzle started to fit together. I finally understood the one thing I deeply needed to understand: how strong and able I was.

Cultivating Self-Esteem by Embracing Perceived Weaknesses

One piece of advice I was given to erase self-doubt was to do positive affirmations and visualization techniques. In the same way self-talk works, repeating positive statements about ourselves can help reshape our mindset and replace negative thoughts with more confident ones. Visualizing ourselves achieving success and reaching our goals can also increase our belief in ourselves and eliminate self-doubt.

This technique helped me differently. It allowed me to see what I really wanted in life and what success meant to me. What was I visualizing if everything was possible? If I was not afraid of failing and was confident in my abilities, what would I do, and who would I be? Visualizing greatly helped me respond to these questions. I now had the motivation I needed to change.

However, it did not really help fix my low self-esteem. To do so, I began to illuminate everything I had accomplished. I became aware of the journey I had taken. When we are excessively caught up in our lives, we tend to forget to pause and look back at our journey. The one we desperately wanted to be short ended up lasting months or years without us even realizing it.

Positive affirmations and visualizations can help alleviate self-doubt and low self-esteem. Still, if we do not honestly believe and realize all the achievements that we have made, it will not work. We stop doubting our abilities when we process everything that we have accomplished one by one.

I was focusing so much on thinking that my conditions were weaknesses that I forgot to see the other side of the coin and how they were also my biggest strength. But slowly, it became more apparent in my mind. Yes, my conditions have been a disadvantage sometimes, but they have made me the person I am today. Would I be so perseverant if I had not been sick? Probably not. Would I be able to cheer for even the most minor things in life if I had not been sick? Not to the extent that I do. Would I be able to face adversity and put myself back on my feet in record time if I had not been sick? No.

It was only when I realized that what I thought to be a weakness was actually a strength that I gained back my self-esteem. It is a lesson that I hope everyone will come to realize. So often, we are so focused on our weaknesses that we are blinded by what they bring to us, how much they make us grow, and how much we learn from them. If we had no weaknesses, we would never be able to evolve.

All the successes you have in life mostly come from overcoming your weaknesses. Instead of berating ourselves for our mistakes or shortcomings, we can acknowledge them, practice forgiveness and understanding, and then learn from them.

As I slowly erased my self-doubt, my worthiness became stronger. That did not happen in one day (once again, sorry for that). The process and the turmoil in my brain between my past and present beliefs fought between each other for weeks in my head. And it would be during one particular event that I would come to realize that I was finally free from my low self-esteem.

Do not give up on the work you need to do to build self-esteem. When you stop doubting your abilities and actively grow your self-esteem, you will start building confidence. You will finally create the confidence you need to live the life you deserve.

What Ultimate Confidence Looked Like for Me

It was in November 2021 that the pieces of the puzzle finally started to fall into place. I slowly became aware of everything I went through and how capable and strong I was. I had managed to go through one sepsis, eight surgeries, a global pandemic, and the loss of my pancreas while continuing to work in a managerial position without being replaced or having to delegate some of my work. I had also gone back to college as a full-time student in an attempt to understand psychology. I was still standing, and after decades of feeling unworthy, I was finally becoming proud of myself.

Going through all these events pushed me to solve the psychological turmoil I had been carrying around for decades. It is so hard to walk and move through life with the heavy burden of not loving ourselves; to depend on others for something that should come from within.

Slowly, my attitude shifted as I realized more about what I had been through and how I had reacted to these events. Isn't it funny that the reason why I developed this syndrome in the first place was actually the one who would set me free?

Remember I told you that it was one specific

moment that made me understand how much more confident I became? Let me now tell you about this event.

November 2021

I finally returned to the office following my surgery. As an extrovert, let's say that working from home was not the best of experiences. I was happy to be back surrounded by my colleagues. But as my self-doubt was slowly being erased, I did not come back as the person I was during my five years working for this company. Nobody could really see how much I had changed as my lack of confidence was thoroughly masked during the past years. But I *was* changed. And I was ready to stop my past behaviors and self-destructive habits. It was my actions that showed me I had finally gained the confidence I needed to thrive.

My salary was one of the first areas I was the most willing to change due to my new realization. Indeed, for years I had accepted a situation I should not have due to my lack of confidence in myself and my work. Despite gaining promotions and responsibilities, my salary did not reflect this growth.

So one day, armed with courage and a buildup of resentment, I must admit, I went to see my CEO to discuss the issue and my future in the company. What I found during this meeting was not what I was initially looking for; it was much more. I did not get the increase I wanted, far from it. But he gave me what I needed the most, even if he did not realize it.

As I entered his office, I had thoroughly prepared my speech on why it was legitimate for me to obtain a salary increase. However, there were a few things I had not been preparing for: my mindset and the real reason why I profoundly wanted a salary increase. Indeed, salary has never been a question of numbers for me but more of value. I am not saying this should be the case; we all have very different perspectives on this matter that are based on what we value. But for me, your salary represents your value in the company. Thus, the more you are paid, the more valuable you are to a company. Titles have no impact on me; you could call me the queen of marketing for all I'd care.

As we started talking, he quickly adopted the speech that had worked very well with me in the past years. You see, in the past, you just needed to question my value and my capacity to do something for me to run back to my desk as fast as a rocket and start to work even harder to try to prove my worth. My behavior was so predictable, I must say. The problem was that I was not this person anymore. As I stood listening to him questioning my capacity to do my job, I could not stop thinking, "Who the hell does he think he is?"

I had worked my ass off to manage the work without asking for help, and business had gone on as usual. I had taken work calls while in my hospital bed. And he was now telling me that I should remember everything they did for me. When this technique would have worked on me even a few months earlier, it did not anymore. This time, I was aware of my capabilities and was mainly proud of everything I had accomplished.

And that's when I decided I would never again let someone determine my value and tell me what I am capable of.

After that meeting, my decision to leave was made. I must say that, to my biggest surprise, he was shocked when I announced it. Unfortunately, it was too late, and no amount of money would have made me stay. He had given me the last slap in the face I needed to finally pursue my dreams. And for this, I am really grateful to him. He gave me the most significant gift by refusing my raise at that time because, in the end, if I had gotten it, I would have stayed in my comfort zone in a job that did not resonate with me anymore. Moreover, I had built so much resentment in the past years on my view of my value in the company that it was beyond repair.

I want to be clear on one thing; I am the only one guilty in this story. It was not my company's fault. Yes, they benefited from my complete lack of trust in myself. But I was the one who had accepted the deal. If I was not happy, I could have just expressed it instead of spending sleepless nights due to rumination. I could have left but chose to stay as the fear of not being up to the task was too big. Despite constantly receiving congratulations from my managers in my work life, I was still crippled by fear of being a fraud. So I stayed in misery instead. I was foolish by expecting them to see my worth when I could not even notice.

We are the author of our own stories. It is our choice to accept the treatment we receive. We can all live in a fantasy world, believing that one day everyone will see our worth and respect us, but unfortunately, that world does not exist. For example, I think everyone should have innate value and respect as humans, but that is not the case. Therefore, as we cannot control how others will act, we need to be confident to step back when we believe we are being unfairly treated. Only we can do it. People can disrespect us, but we can choose not to accept it.

We are so afraid of what we will lose that we would rather stay in unhealthy and unhappy situations or relationships. But life is a gamble. When we leave something, we never know what we will find. We need to trust our ability to stand back up. And if we keep analyzing our life as an outsider would, we are better able to see the many times we got back on our feet. Was it scary? Yes. But we did it.

Gaining confidence in myself helped me fix another symptom of imposter syndrome affecting my life: the constant need of people pleasing. So for all the fellow people-pleasers out there, the next chapter is for you.

6.

Stop
People
Pleasing

"If you live for peoples acceptance, you will die from their rejection."

- Lecrae

W hat would we do without our people-pleasing habit? I wonder. There is an uncontrollable urge to say "yes" to every request that comes our way, even if deep down we want to say "no." It is a strange feeling. On the one hand, it gives us this rush of dopamine for helping someone, while on the other hand, it makes us feel frustrated and angry at ourselves.

The Art of People Pleasing

Let's say a colleague from another department just asked us to help on a project as they are leaving for vacation and won't have time to finish before they go. It has nothing to do with our job, but none of their teams can take on the extra workload. Neither can we, for the matter. But if we say "no," what will they think? Will they be mad? Will this mean I am a terrible person? Will this show that I am a bad teammate? Will they believe that I am selfish?

As all these questions pop into our minds, we decide to say "yes." This decision will make us lose track of our actual work, and we will need to work extra hours to accommodate it. Our brains start to look for excuses for why we will not be able to do it. We look for the most extreme one as panic settles inside us. We find one that might be a bit extreme but will prevent them from questioning it. We repeat in our head the words; we are ready to say "no." And then, as our mouths open, these words come out instead: "Of course, I will be happy to help!"

Here it goes again; we have said "yes" to something we did not want.

We can blame them for putting ourselves in this position. We can even start to build resentment toward them. Why ask me when I have nothing to do with the job? Every legitimate person to take on the task said "no," and I now find myself in this situation. But in the end, we are the ones who said "yes." Because, contrary to others, we have mastered the art of people pleasing.

We are the go-to person if someone needs a favor. If someone needs someone to babysit their sick cat or a place to sleep for a few nights, they can always ask us. We are the most generous people with our time, money, and belongings; we are always ready to help. We sound like exceptional people, right? What people do not know is that we might become profoundly depressed and unhappy as a result of our constant need to please. We start to resent ourselves whenever we say "yes" to something we do not want to do. We never learned to say "no."

This example is one of many where we find ourselves in this dreadful situation just because we have not learned to say "no." At least, I was in these types of situations quite often. Despite hours of practicing how to say "no," I could never find myself saying it. I would come up with crazy excuses for why I could not do something, just to diminish the scary two letter word. But the uncomfortable feeling that followed was enough to make me say "yes." The problem was that the sense of anxiousness, resentment, and anger about myself was even more significant, but in other ways, it was easier to accept.

Boundaries Are Necessary for Healthy Hearts and Minds

There is another side of people pleasing that we tend to forget: It is our inability to clearly say what we think or state our opinions. As we do not want to compromise the possibility of receiving validation from others, we deny our true thoughts, which fuels the imposter inside us even more.

However, failing to set boundaries in these situations might cause us to lose more than our time as it can lead us to resentment and a loss of self-respect.

To truly respect others, we must first learn how to respect ourselves and our own boundaries. We need to learn to communicate openly and honestly with those around us and stand up for what we believe in. I know that one is tricky. We do not often learn how to communicate effectively without letting our emotions get the best of us. And just because we are scared of how the person will react, we have learned to shut our mouths and people please instead.

But we should all remember that it is not selfish or rude to take care of ourselves and prioritize our needs. What showing respect for ourselves will guarantee is having better and worthier relationships.

People pleasing, also known as being a people pleaser, is the tendency to put others' needs and desires above your own to avoid confrontation or disapproval. This behavior can often lead to sacrificing personal boundaries and neglecting self-care to please others.

While this behavior may seem kind and considerate on the surface, people pleasing can actually create feelings of resentment and anger toward both oneself and others. It can also lead to difficulty setting and maintaining personal boundaries and a lack of assertiveness in communication and decision-making.

Having a lack of confidence in yourself and living as an imposter most likely made you become an expert at people pleasing. And how could it not? People pleasing is a way to gain love, acceptance, and approval from others while avoiding conflict. It becomes a coping mechanism for fear of not being good enough.

By saying "yes" to all the various demands, we avoid putting ourselves in situations where there could be conflict or disapproval. It also makes us falsely believe that people will love us. However, constantly putting others before ourselves can lead to feeling resentful and exhausted. It can be a hard habit to break. I realized the detrimental effects of people pleasing during an event that threw me into a level of anxiety that I had rarely felt. But as I rewound different events in my life, I saw how these small, unwanted instances of saying "yes" trapped me in unwanted situations over the years.

The Consequences of People Pleasing

I always admired my colleague Shannon. She had this powerful ability to say "no" in an authoritative manner in situations where I was sweating like a wimp just thinking about saying "no." However, I must admit she was the smarter of us two. She had defined boundaries that I did not, and therefore, people knew that and did not come to her to ask for favors in areas outside of her work.

I was the total opposite. I always said "yes." And what happens when we always say "yes?" We train people to come to us as a result of our behavior. I am not saying they are manipulative people. Still, people quickly identify those willing to be used (the ones who are trying to compensate, who want to please, and who lack self-confidence) and will abuse their need for approval. And that is how we find ourselves trapped in an unwanted cycle once again. And like everything, it will never change unless we break the pattern and change how people see us, even with how uncomfortable it can be.

The awkwardness and fear of what could happen if we decide to say "no" may stop us from acting. We tried once, and the anxiety that followed made us want to step back. But let me tell you something: At this moment, we are being fooled by our brain, which is doing the one thing it likes the most—staying in its comfort zone. And just like that, in the few seconds we have to think about our answer, we forget the negative feeling we also experience when we unwillingly say "yes."

Maybe you will experience one event where your people-pleasing attitude will be so detrimental to your mental state that you will finally understand the adverse effects of people pleasing.

Learning Things the Hard Way

I had one of these events. I stupidly placed myself in a situation where my people-pleasing attitude would cause me more sweat than ever.

I was selling my car and had agreed with the buyer to meet late afternoon to proceed with the paperwork. In Dubai, the procedure is done in a dedicated governmental facility, and all purchases are made in cash. By doing so, they avoid the issues of nonpayment and ensure that everything goes smoothly.

As the meeting time was approaching, I took to the road and started driving to the facility. After 10 minutes of driving, I received a message from the buyer. She explained that she had been unable to withdraw the entire amount in cash as she had a limit and therefore needed my bank details so she could do a wire transfer instead.

My heart pounded as I faced the two choices I had. I could protect myself by saying "no," as a wire would likely take days to arrive in my account. It was already Friday evening, and the weekend meant no bank transfers would be processed. Moreover, as all transactions were asked to be made in cash, I would lose all legal protection once I signed the change of ownership agreement in the evening. That was the smart choice to make. Or I could say "yes," take the risk of not receiving the money, and have to get into a legal battle if something went wrong.

The most rational person would have chosen the first option. I, myself, would have advised anyone to do so. Even if Dubai is famous for its securities and strict penalties in case of fraudulent actions, we still choose safety over risk.

Did I follow my own advice? Of course, I didn't. As I read the message, my brain started buzzing as I tried to make my decision. I knew I wanted to politely say "no" as it was the safest solution, but on the other hand, I thought, "She is going to believe I do not trust her." It was a silly thing to think as we cannot presume to trust someone we don't know. As my lawyer friend later told me when I explained the story (to his greatest despair), she would have completely understood if I had decided to wait for the money to be in my account before proceeding with the sale. But as saying "no" was more challenging than "yes," I sent my bank details while spending the next 30 minutes googling all the ways someone could fake a screenshot, cancel a wire transfer, and so on.

While I sat in the facility with her waiting to do the paperwork, my anxiety was rising, and a feeling of uneasiness invaded me. On one side, I knew the risk was low as she did not seem like a professional scam artist, and I had proof of the transfer. But on the other side, I could not stop thinking about what I could lose if I were wrong. As I left her with her new car, the feelings of fear, frustration, anxiety, and stress only increased. I knew that the chances of quickly putting my mind to ease were slim as the weekend would mean that the transfer would most likely arrive on a Monday morning.

It was going to be a long weekend.

In an attempt to reassure myself, I called my lawyer friend to tell him the story. Let's say that calling a lawyer to tell him that I had given over ownership of my car before receiving the funds is not a great idea. His legal mind did not at all put me at ease; quite the opposite, I will say. So as my brain desperately needed to be placed at ease, I called my sister, who had a much more human point of view on the matter. It did help, but it did not stop me from checking at least 10 times if the car's new owner had cut me off from message services, a sign that I believed would show potential fraud.

I woke up the following day feeling even worse than the night before. My sister's wise words did not help ease the stress. As I went for my morning walk in an attempt to clear my mind, I was utterly incapable of reducing my anxiety. I had not experienced that much stress in years and felt it in all areas of my body. My blood sugar kept rising at the same speed as my fears. The thought of spending the weekend in this state of mind frightened me. How could I have been that stupid? The uneasiness of saying "no" was small compared to what I was experiencing now. I was so mad at myself for inflicting this situation on me.

And at 8:36 a.m. that same day, I received the most relieving message: one from the bank announcing the receipt of the transfer. I felt so relieved that sweat of relief dropped from my face as my heart started pounding and my hands were shaking.

It was once again an extreme situation that does not happen every day. But it taught me a great lesson: the impact people pleasing has on our minds and bodies. Because the case was extreme, I could only see how it negatively impacted me. But even less extreme situations lead us to negative emotions; we just do not realize their impacts.

By unwillingly accepting to constantly put others' needs before our own, we put our bodies under stressors that affect us in the long run. We also may experience anger and frustration as we do not have the time or energy to tend to our own needs. Our willpower to accomplish something for ourselves will be diminished as all of our mental energy is spent on others.

Psychological Costs

There are other costs besides physiological ones associated with living as a people pleaser. Some psychologists suggest that we could lose our sense of identity as we are not living our own life but living to please others all the time. It can give us a feeling of emptiness or dissatisfaction with life. Ultimately, living as a people pleaser can result in an overall loss of emotional well-being and happiness.

One of the other downfalls of people pleasing is your loss of decision-making abilities. We have accepted others' choices for so long that we cannot remember if we would make a different choice if given a chance. This leads to even more self-doubt and low self-esteem and confidence.

Do you see how all our bad habits fuel each other and result in a spiral of adverse effects?

The Costs to Our Relationships

People pleasing can also negatively impact our relationships. Constantly accommodating others may lead to feelings of resentment and anger toward them, even though we were the ones who put their needs before our own. This can lead to strained relationships and difficulties in setting boundaries with those around us. Some may also take our kindness for granted after a time, leading to even more resentful feelings as we feel that they are taking advantage of us.

I have chosen carefully to add the word "unwillingly"

before "yes" as I do not believe that never helping others is a good thing either. We live in communities, and helping out our peers when they need it, even if we are not happy about it sometimes, is a great human value. Occasionally, we need to accept the family dinner we do not want to go to or watch a friend's play, even if we hate sitting in a theater for hours. It is when it becomes extreme and repetitive that it becomes an issue.

People pleasing can lead us to change our life path. Some people may accept going into a career that they do not like to please their parents. We may sacrifice our projects for the ones of others. Like everything in life, it is a balance, and being on one extreme or the other is something we should avoid.

Also, we should never forget that saying "yes" to something means saying "no" to something else. We all have the same allotment of time in a day; unfortunately, that factor is unchangeable. When we say "yes" to something, we sacrifice our time and energy that could have been used for something else. This is when we should strive to change.

But even when we know that and we scream it to our friends when they face these situations, we are not taking a dose of our own medicine. We have become professional people pleasers for many reasons, and until we understand the real reason why we cannot say "no," this habit is hard to change.

Why Do We Become People Pleasers?

It is a normal human need to feel accepted, but for some of us, the need to please others is so strong that we will sacrifice our own needs, dreams, and even our identity to be accepted.

The need to be part of a group is written in our DNA. In ancient times, one's survival was dependent on our tribe. The tribe offered protection and resources to its members; if you were alienated from your tribe, it was a death sentence.

Today our circumstances may differ, but the need for acceptance is still strong. We start to form bonds from the moment we are born, and meaningful relationships are essential to our human existence. According to Perel (n.d.), psychotherapist and relationship expert, "The quality of our relationships determines the quality of our lives" (para. 1). We fear being alone and being rejected is painful; these are all normal human emotions and reactions.

But there is a dark side to this need for acceptance.

Ironically, the extreme need to please others comes from an inability to value ourselves. We feel that others judge us by how useful we are, and to be validated by them, we need to please them constantly. But why did we become extremists about it?

People Pleasing Can Be Rooted in Childhood Experiences

My low self-esteem and feeling of unworthiness were not only in terrible shape due to my conditions, but they were also fueled during my teenage years. My mother had passed away, and my father, being a "real catch" in the dating scene, did not take long to find love again. After 11 years of supporting my mother in her fight against cancer to the best of his abilities, he was finally free to start living again.

His new partner was living in Paris when we were in the suburbs, so he went to live with her, and I stayed with my siblings in our family home. Soon, they went on to live their lives, and I stayed alone in our beautiful, three-story house.

Now that I was the only one left, my father's visits became less and less frequent. At that age, I interpreted the situation differently than I do now as an adult. I had lost my mother, and the only other person that was supposed to love me no matter what did not wish to spend time with me. That must have meant that I had nothing to offer and was not worthy of love.

As I stayed alone for days and weeks due to my condition, I could not keep these thoughts of unworthiness from invading my brain. They remained my companion for years, even when I finally understood that my father's behavior was not about me.

I can't imagine how he must have felt when he found

himself the sole provider of three teenage kids. He had always been the family's financial provider as my mother was a stay-at-home mom. But my mother took care of us in all aspects of our lives since we were born. She was the one who decided on our education, supported us in our extracurricular activities, bought gifts for our birthdays and Christmas, reprimanded us when we were misbehaving, and so on. She knew us better than anyone. So when she passed away, his world was shackled as he realized he had no idea how to manage it. Suddenly, he had three grieving teenage kids to handle, and he was a total beginner, not a very good situation to find yourself in.

I can still remember the fear in his eyes as my mother's body was still lying lifeless in our house, and I asked him with tears in mine, "Who is going to take me shopping now?" He responded without an ounce of confidence, "I will."

When you add up the fact that he had supported my mother in her sickness for more than a decade, something courageous, he saw fleeing as the only solution. He just wanted to get back a sense of life and finally live the life he had been unable to live for so many years. And I am glad he did. We are now closer than ever, as he realized in my mid-20s his mistakes, and I discovered his motives. Although he feels immense sadness for the past and my current challenges, he is now a supportive figure in my life.

His abandonment was not about me or who I was as a person; it resulted from his fear and wish to live his life.

Of course, understanding this as a teenage kid in the heat of the moment was complicated, if not impossible. So I began to want to please people even more. I was desperately trying to seek the love and attention of others, as I believed it would bring me the love I was seeking. In my mind, I also developed the idea that if I made myself irreplaceable, people would not be able to abandon me anymore. So it became my thought pattern for years until I understood I was worthy, especially in my father's eyes. When I let go of my feeling of unworthiness and doubts about myself, I could heal.

Many factors can contribute to becoming a people pleaser. Often, early childhood experiences play a role in shaping our behavior and desire for approval from others. For example, growing up in an environment where one's self-worth is tied to meeting others' expectations can lead to constantly seeking validation from others. Additionally, low self-esteem and fear of rejection can also drive someone to prioritize others' needs over their own. That is why this step comes after building confidence. If you still lack confidence in yourself, erasing the habit of people pleasing will be hard.

Fears, Personalities, and Boundaries

In her book *Captivate*, Van Edwards (2017), founder of *Science of People*, explains that anxiety and neurotic tendencies are prevalent among people pleasers due to their intense fear of rejection. This anxiety can often lead to an inability to set boundaries, resulting in burnout, and resentment toward those who take advantage of their willingness to please.

Does that mean that certain personality types are more inclined to become people pleasers?

According to a study by Byerly et al. (2022), those who scored high on agreeableness and neuroticism were more likely to prioritize others' needs over their own. Meanwhile, those who scored high on conscientiousness were more likely to prioritize their own needs. So if your personality naturally favors pleasing people, that's okay; I am part of that club too. It is a behavior that can definitely be changed with effort and awareness. We just need to learn how to say "no."

Van Edwards (2017) also notes that by learning assertiveness skills and setting healthy boundaries, people pleasers can break free from the cycle of constantly putting others' needs before their own. It may be difficult, but it ultimately leads to increased self-respect and healthier relationships.

So even though undertaking this journey sounds doubtful, we have to learn how to say "no" and start placing value on our own needs. Remember, pleasing others is not worth sacrificing our own happiness and well-being.

The Art of Saying "No"

The awkwardness and fear of what could happen if you decide to say "no" may stop you from acting. However, it is by living through this awkwardness that we learn.

Learn to Say "No"

One of the biggest challenges in learning to say "no" is overcoming the desire to please others and the quick dopamine it brings us. Let's admit it, we like receiving compliments, feeling needed and wanted, and being respected for being a "yes" person. However, constantly saying "yes" to others can lead to overextending ourselves and ultimately causing stress and burnout. But as we have seen in the previous section, failing to do so could greatly affect our lives.

It's important to recognize that saying no does not make you a bad or selfish person. Setting boundaries and prioritizing our own well-being is necessary for healthy relationships and personal growth. To help you under-stand this idea, think about how many times some people have told you "no." Maybe it frustrated you as this concept is unfamiliar to you, but in the end, you accepted their decisions and moved on.

The quote, "Say no to be successful," is accurate for many people. You must give precedence to your priorities and do the best work possible. If it means that to do so, you need to refuse something, it's okay; you will never regret saying no later, while you will regret not doing what you wanted to do.

If you spend your time saying "yes" to everything, you will mostly lose in the long run.

So, the next time you find yourself in one of these situations, try the following:

- Turn your tongue 10 times in your mouth before responding.
- Take this time to think about your capacity to accept (because time is not flexible) and what you will have to say "no" to if you do say "yes."
- If you determine you are happy to help and have the time, go ahead.
- However, politely decline if you do not.
- We all think we have to give an excuse if we decide to say "no" to something. You should not explain your decision; a "no, I will not be able to help" is enough. We must stop wasting our energy always trying to justify our choices and decisions.

Also, it is best to say "no" to any requests that make us feel uncomfortable, obligated, or "put on the spot." We are all familiar with the situation when someone asks us a very awkward question, most often a personal one, and even if we really do not want to respond, we do so in fear of being rejected from the clan. We are so afraid to be laughed at even if we despise being placed in this situation. That is bullshit. I know we have this uncontrollable feeling of belonging, but we should ask ourselves which group we actually want to be a part of. Do we want to associate with people who will not understand us, or do we want to be surrounded by those who have our best interests at heart and will support us in whatever decisions we make?

The key to breaking away from a people-pleasing mentality is setting boundaries that we feel comfortable with.

People pleasing can also make us accept or approve of what someone else says when we disagree. We are so afraid of confrontation that we deny our opinion to ensure we do not hurt or make someone else angry. But by doing so, we lose our identity, and we can even start doubting our decisions and beliefs. If we want to keep our confidence, it is crucial to stand up for our opinions and trust them. After discussing the matter with the person, we can always change our mind—it is what wise people do—but we should communicate our thoughts effectively in the first place.

Practicing assertiveness can help combat people-pleasing tendencies. This involves expressing your needs and opinions clearly and confidently without apologizing or downplaying them. It's also important to recognize and challenge any negative thoughts or beliefs that may fuel people-pleasing behavior.

Saying "no" can feel uncomfortable initially, but it gets easier with practice.

The Art of Setting Boundaries

Boundaries are meant to protect our feelings, mind, body, and well-being.

The first step in setting boundaries is to establish them in your head. Decide what you are willing to do or concede and what not. Be clear and specific in your thoughts. The next step is to inform others of your decisions. You do not need to explain yourself; you can still be friendly and kind while setting boundaries.

For example, if a friend asks you to go out on Saturday even though you would rather stay in and chill, decide if you are willing to attend and if not, muster up the courage to say it. We all have been guilty of unwillingly saying "yes" to a plan and then later trying to find the biggest excuse to cancel. We will spend days thinking about how to get out of the obligation while we could have just been honest from the beginning.

Sometimes, we will push ourselves and go, which will, most of the time, result in an early exit. I know it all too well. My friends called me "Cinderella" as I always quietly exited the party before midnight. I am an early sleeper and going to loud clubs until 3 a.m. is not my cup of tea. I could refuse to go, but as I did not want to disappoint, I always said "yes." As I no longer care to be rejected by my fellow "party" friends, I no longer force myself to go unless it is a special event.

Don't Make Excuses

The biggest mistake we make when refusing something is trying to find an excuse. We think that it will actually help us justify why we are saying "no," but it only allows the other person to find an argument to convince us. We are even the ones doing it sometimes (we should definitely stop that). When someone tells us "no," we might respond with something like, "Come on, it's going to be fun!" in an attempt to make them change their minds. Instead, when the person asks why you cannot attend, you do not need to explain; a short "thank you, but I cannot accept" will suffice.

Relationships Should Be in Balance

Be mindful that some people may have been taking advantage of your generosity and will not like your new boundaries. These are the same people that ask for favors or help but are always unavailable when you need something from them in return. Remember, a relationship is a give and take; if one person is always giving and the other is always on the receiving end, it is not healthy. Social media allows for many "connections" but creates pseudo self-esteem that is misinterpreted and ultimately hollow. Being friends with people who do not deserve our friendship is not worth it. It is better to have fewer good friends than many "fake" friends.

Respect Your Time and Energy

Another boundary that will give you more control over your life is not always being available to take phone calls or answer texts. If you need downtime at night, keep your phone silent and only attend to calls and messages in the morning. People will soon learn not to disturb you at certain times. It is something that I implemented at work and has been very successful.

One day, one of my colleagues told me how tired she was of receiving calls and texts in the late evening (thank you, time difference). On my side, I never had this issue because I had set this boundary from the beginning. When people are used to being able to contact you at any time, they will keep going until you put a stop to it. Of course, if there was an emergency, I would respond and help. But most of the time, there is not. The person is just conveniently using your lack of boundaries.

By implementing boundaries, people will learn to respect your time and energy. It will also help to reduce stress and improve your self-esteem. Setting boundaries can also lead to better communication within relationships and friendships. So don't be afraid to say "no" or disappoint someone; it is for your own well-being and the health of the relationship. Be brave, stand up for yourself, and set those boundaries. Your future self will thank you.

. . .

Sometimes, I still encounter the residue of my long-term people-pleasing habit. I caught myself feeling the urge to offer my help to people I don't even know. It is great to want to help, but when you do not have time to do it properly, it is not fair to the person nor yourself. So I learned the powerful effect of turning my tongue a thousand times in my mouth. It is by far, the most effective technique I found to fix my habit of saying "yes" to everything.

7.

Own
Your
Successes

"I find that the harder I work, the more luck I seem to have."

- Thomas Jefferson

W hen you suffer from imposter syndrome and feel that your success is not because of your hard work, it is easy to blame luck. But how much does luck really have to do with our successes? Can we really attribute everything to luck or do our decisions, work, and behavior affect our successes?

You might already have the answers as you think about these questions. But let's dig deeper into these questions so we can really make an informed decision.

The Place of Luck in Our Lives

We cannot deny the luck factor in our life as luck does exist. I am a very lucky person. I grew up in France, a country that provides free education and prides itself on freedom and equality. My parents did everything they could to offer me the best chance in life. I never had any financial worries. This was pure luck. My life would have been entirely different if I had not been born in this family and the western world. I realize that I have an unfair advantage compared to many other people in this world. And denying it wouldn't be a very educated stance.

According to Kahneman (2011), humans tend to diminish the effect of luck in their successes and magnify the role of skill or talent. However, luck plays a significant role in our achievements and should not be overlooked. In his book *Thinking, Fast and Slow*, Kahneman (2011) discusses the concept of "the illusion of validity," where individuals overestimate their ability to predict future events and outcomes. This can lead us to underestimate the impact of luck and random chance on our successes.

Furthermore, research has shown that luck plays a larger role in success for those at the top of their field. A study by Pluchino et al. (2018) found that among individuals at the very top of extremely competitive environments, luck accounts for a significant fraction of outcomes.

While hard work and perseverance are important factors in achieving success, it is important to recognize the role of luck and chance. By acknowledging luck as a factor in our successes, we can remain humble and grateful for the opportunities that have been presented to us. It also opens us up to considering alternate paths and alternatives in difficult situations, rather than fixating on a singular "lucky" outcome. Luck may always be a mysterious force but acknowledging its influence can lead to a more balanced and grateful perspective on our achievements.

The Consequences of Attributing Everything to Luck

Is luck the only thing at play? Luck can bring us opportunities we need to succeed but seizing this opportunity will depend on us. For example, Bill Gates explained how lucky he was to attend a school with a computer, something scarce back then, and how it played a massive role in his success. However, his hard work made him develop and use his skills to seize opportunities and achieve success. There were hundreds of other students in his school, but they did not end up creating the biggest software company in the world. So, yes, luck may bring us opportunities, but it is up to us to work hard and make good use of those opportunities if we want to achieve success.

A friend told me how lucky I was to have nice legs not so long ago. And for the first time, I did not respond with the typical "yes, thank you very much; I am a very lucky person" because it would have been lying to her and letting her believe that she had no power over this. It is not luck. I have trained every morning as soon as I wake up for the past two years. My genetics have nothing to do with this; trust me, if I stop working out, those legs will disappear as fast as they arrived. By believing luck is the only root of success, we put ourselves in a mindset promoting inaction.

Yes, I am very lucky; I have a personality that positively impacts my ability to manage my conditions. I am naturally a very happy, joyful, and optimistic (maybe sometimes a little bit too much, but that is another story) person. But it was not all luck. Realizing the parts of luck and work in our successes is key. I, too, attributed too many achievements to luck when it was only a part of the percentage—the others were work and effort.

In 2020, I started working out every day; I learned everything I could about my conditions to try to find solutions. I never pitied myself, and I made sure I ate the correct food even if it was not always easy. I moved to another country to get the job of my dreams, and I never gave up, even when I faced enormous challenges with my health. I became self-aware and took responsibility for my actions, good and bad.

Your Mindset Matters

We should not solely rely upon luck in our lives. First, it can put us in "victim" mode.

Attributing every success or accomplishment to luck can lead us to inaction as we feel powerless in front of situations. We may believe that everything is out of our control and that there is nothing we can do to improve our circumstances. Second, it makes us blind to our strengths and abilities. So by not recognizing what we have achieved, we put ourselves at risk of self-doubt and low self-esteem.

We will remain in a fixed mindset by not recognizing that we have the power to achieve what we want. Whatever we try to accomplish in life, our mindset will define our success rate. And there is a concept that every imposter should understand: fixed versus growth mindset. In her book *Mindset*, Dweck (2006) talks about the importance of having a growth mindset. A growth mindset is the belief that we can improve and grow with effort. People with a growth mindset don't give up easily because they believe that they can always get better. So, if we want to achieve our goals, we must have positive self-talk and tell ourselves that we can do it. Remember that all the limits you have in life are the ones in your head.

Taking ownership of our successes also means we should take ownership of our failures and mistakes. I think this last part is crucial. If we keep attributing our successes to luck and our failures to ourselves, how are we going to be able to chase our dreams? Because we are only guaranteed to lose all the time in this configuration.

For one minute, think logically about this; we do not tell someone who constantly has issues at work because of non-performance being fired was "bad luck." We (and they, hopefully) know that their actions led to their dismissal. The same is true for our achievements. Why would we give "luck" credit if we know that we have worked hard for the promotion or raise?

We also need to change our beliefs surrounding the

success of others. So often, we hear someone say, "Ok, they succeeded, but they do not deserve their success; they are just lucky." And please, we are among honest people here. Do not tell me that you have never said or thought that. If we analyze the situation in which we found ourselves thinking that, we were most likely making that conclusion rooted in jealousy.

I will be honest and admit that I did find myself thinking this negative belief. But I was wrong. Because even if the person has been the luckiest person on Earth and got what I wanted and I did not, I should still be happy for them. But I was mostly setting myself up for failure, thinking I had no power over my luck. By ignoring this person's work, I set myself in a situation of learned helplessness.

Learned Helplessness

I discovered the term learned helplessness not so long ago. Learned helplessness is the belief that we can't do anything to change a situation. This can keep people from taking action, even when they have the power to do so. Imposter syndrome is a form of learned helplessness. We believe we are not good enough or qualified to do something, so we stay in our misery. We can even say that sometimes it is easier to do so. It is so comfortable and cozy to stay in what we know, even if it harms us. Our brain doesn't want to change because it fears the unknown. So we just keep repeating the same mistakes over and over again.

The only way to break this vicious cycle is to take a leap of faith and try something new. It might be scary at first but trust me; it will be worth it in the end. You will be surprised by your own strength and capabilities. Take a chance and see what life has to offer outside of your comfort zone. You might be surprised at how great it can be. Your brain will thank you for it.

Instead of waiting for good luck to come our way, let's take ownership of our actions and decisions. Let's promise to strive to improve and better ourselves constantly. A famous saying changed my mentality forever: "I have not failed if I have learned."

Because if we never fail, we never learn, so maybe we should also celebrate our failures. I hope you will take calculated risks and make proactive choices. In doing so, you will be more likely to create opportunities for success rather than just hoping luck falls into your lap.

Remember, success is not only a matter of luck. It is the result of hard work, dedication, and determination. We can't control all aspects of our lives, but at least we can try our best to work on the ones we can.

The Misconception of Talent

Talent is often cited as the reason for someone's success. But is there such a thing as talent? Or do we live in complete denial? Are we screwed if we do not have this inherited talent? For sure, you cannot deny the talent of some geniuses. Mozart composed his first symphony at the age of eight. I mean, let's admire this achievement! If you had asked me to write a symphony at this age, the only result would have been my family's immense displeasure (and for a good reason!). And I think I can confidently say that most of you are more like me than Mozart. But can we become talented at something even if we have no inclination to it?

Psychologist researcher Angela Duckworth (2016) can help us answer this question. In her book *Grit*, she claims that the key to success is not talent but grit. It's about having passion and perseverance toward long-term goals despite any obstacles or failures along the way. And it's a trait that can be cultivated with effort and hard work. So instead of constantly searching for this elusive talent, maybe we should focus on developing our grit and determination.

Talent may play a small part in success, but it is not the determining factor. So next time someone tells you that you are not talented enough to do something, remember: Talent is just a myth. Take a step back and think about the thousands of hours you have dedicated to your craft and tell them. Success comes with grit and hard work. And who knows? Maybe one day we can all compose symphonies like Mozart (just not as fast).

In a recent interview, Ed Sheeran played one of the first recordings of him singing. Let's say that it was not as polished and beautiful as his current hits. By doing so, he wanted to show that his hard practice, learning, and improvement made him become the musician we know today, not a naturally born talent. So why don't we do the same? Let's stop searching for talent and start searching for grit. That is where true success lies.

Duckworth was not the only one to research the concept of inherited talent. Many experts argue that success is not determined by natural talent alone. It requires hard work, dedication, and practice to reach a level of mastery in any field or skill. In fact, this concept has even been studied and proven in psychology through the "10,000-Hour Rule," popularized by Malcolm Gladwell (2011). This rule suggests that it takes 10,000 hours of practice to become an expert or master in a particular field. This means that success is not dependent on talent alone but rather a combination of personal effort and opportunity.

Yes, You Do Have Talents

And now I see you coming at me: Yes, that's great, Coline, but I do not have any talents. I'm sorry to say it, but I do not think that it is possible. We all have skills and qualities that come for free with the human package. However, the ability to recognize and have faith in them does not come with it. This sometimes requires some challenging self-awareness work if you cannot see them. Except if you have a very extreme personality disorder like sociopathy, and in this case, I do not think you would be reading this book.

Indeed, you are endowed with qualities. However, you might not recognize them and how they have helped you out in your life. Instead, you might focus on the ones you do not have naturally and envy the people who have those you desperately want. It is a bit like the concept that when we have curly hair, we want it to be straight and vice versa.

This was the case for me with my friend Marine. She is the complete opposite of me when it comes to personality. Where she is a very thoughtful and thorough person with attention to detail and the embodiment of calmness, I am as impulsive as a bull let loose in the arena, running toward its target without overthinking. So let's say that when we first started working together, our diverse personalities had trouble adjusting to each other until we realized how they were complementary, making our duo work really well.

When long-term strategy needed to be done, Marine was the perfect person to take it on. I was in charge when we needed to act fast and adapt quickly. Often, I have wished to have some of Marine's personality traits. I admired her ability to take the time to develop her ideas and the balance she achieved in her life when clearly, it required extreme effort for me to do the same. And not so long ago, she told me how she wished she could act as quickly and fast as I can.

We both recognize the talents in each of us. We just can't naturally have everything we want in life, but we can work for it. We both support one another in working toward what we want from each other, and I am grateful to have her by my side.

So if you genuinely believe you have been stripped of talents and qualities in life, engage in a more profound analysis of yourself. An excellent way to do it is to write down all your accomplishments. We tend to focus so much on the failures that we forget all the times we got it right.

So acknowledge your hard work and commitment, and jot down the targets you have achieved or the results of a project you were working on. When you doubt your abilities, open up this "brag book" to remind yourself that you have worked hard for a long time to get where you are. It never was just luck.

By becoming self-aware of your achievements, you will realize how far you have come and feel confident about what you can still achieve if you put yourself into it.

And sometimes, it might be good to indulge in some celebrations.

Celebrate Your Successes and Accept Compliments

The benefits of celebrating our achievements are many. A boost in confidence is one such benefit. By sharing and celebrating with family or colleagues, we are validating our achievement. It reminds us of what it took to get there and how hard we worked.

Celebrating our successes also allows us to thank those who helped us achieve them. Seeing others celebrate our success will validate that we accomplished it through hard work and not just by luck.

But should we celebrate all our successes? Celebrating our achievements can help us see the milestone we have accomplished thanks to our hard work. But is it good for us to celebrate everything? It is a question that popped into my head not so long ago after listening to one of Andrew Huberman's podcast episodes on the reward system.

According to Huberman (2022), our brains have a reward system that releases dopamine when we accomplish something. This dopamine release reinforces the behavior that led to that achievement and motivates us to continue on the same path. However, if we constantly celebrate every small achievement, our brains may become desensitized to the dopamine release, and it will no longer motivate us as effectively.

After learning about this theory, I wanted to see if I had been the victim of it. I dug into my memories and realized how being in one extreme or the other hurt my motivation. When there were too many celebrations over small things, I became less motivated to keep working on the project as the rewards became less and less effective (we are very ungrateful creatures sometimes). However, motivation was also a real struggle if I had no reward at all. I saw it when I became diabetic. I quickly realized that having no reward despite extreme efforts to manage the condition was detrimental.

When we accomplish a big milestone at work, we

receive some kind of reward: recognition, status, or pay raise, and it is up to us to accept it. When you live with a chronic condition, your only reward is at best feeling "normal."

Nobody is here to congratulate you for being "normal." And it was burdensome to me. I was fighting hard to manage my conditions, and I had nothing motivating me to continue except long-term effects that I could not foresee. But I understood that if someone told me how great I was doing every day, I would be less inclined to maintain the efforts. I needed a compromise. So now, every six months, when I receive my blood test results, I will make a celebration out of it and force the person next to me (sorry for that) to cheer with me.

It can be helpful to acknowledge and celebrate our achievements, as it can boost our self-esteem and motivation. However, constantly focusing on rewards can also lead to a fixed mindset where we prioritize the outcome over the process and the effort put into achieving it. It's important to strike a balance and take time to recognize our hard work while also continuing to challenge ourselves and strive for growth.

On a neurological level, the reward system in our brain can be triggered by external rewards, such as praise or money, but also by internal factors like feeling accomplished or proud of ourselves. This release of feel-good chemicals can reinforce positive behaviors and drive us to repeat them in the future.

In sum, celebrating our successes can be beneficial,

but it's also important to continue pushing ourselves and not become overly fixated on rewards.

Learning to Accept Compliments

I always admire individuals that gracefully accept compliments. My cheeks will get as red as a tomato whenever someone sends a compliment my way. A couple of months back, I found myself in this exact situation in front of 100 students. I had just given a speech to business school students on my career journey, going from a university dropout, to finally graduating, to entrepreneurship in the event industry, to a managerial position in corporate life, and soon to jump into the realm of publishing. And it happened. At the end of my address, one of the teachers stood up to congratulate me on my perseverance and unconventional journey (especially for the French standard). I did not know what to do with myself. My fuchsia dress had completely spread its color into my face.

Why is it so hard to accept compliments?

In an attempt to get better at this, I came back home and decided to look for some tips from experts. Vanessa Van Edwards is definitely the go-to person to understand human behaviors and learn how to change some of our most awkward ones.

And soon enough, I found an article on her website that helped me understand what I could do to get better at receiving compliments.

She suggests four simple steps to accepting a compliment (Van Edwards, 2022):

1. Say "thank you." This may sound obvious, but it is important to remember to say these two simple words instead of deflecting or changing the subject.
2. Repeat the compliment back to the giver. This allows for clarification and shows that you truly heard what they said about you.
3. Take a moment to savor the compliment and allow yourself to feel good about it. Don't immediately brush off or dismiss what was said about you.
4. Return the compliment to the giver if possible. This helps build rapport and creates a positive interaction for both parties involved.

I decided to try these steps the next time I faced a similar situation. I must admit that repeating the compliment back was the hardest to do as it makes you feel pretentious. As shameful as it might feel to accept, be grateful and happy to receive a compliment. Trust me, try responding, "Thanks, I know I did great," and you will see how hard it is. It is like we have been programmed not to be happy when someone compliments us. And if you are like me, you will also react strangely if someone tells you something like this after you have complimented them. It is like an unwritten social rule that celebrating our success is conceited (one we should debunk as a society).

Practicing these steps can help make accepting compliments a little less daunting. Remember, someone took the time to say something nice about us, so let's allow ourselves to feel good about it and practice gratitude. It is not something that happens every day (at least not for me!).

Next time someone compliments you, try these steps and see how it feels. I became better at it with practice, and even if my cheeks still turn red, I am grateful for the reason. You may surprise yourself with how confident and poised you can be in accepting a compliment.

Happy accepting!

By now, I hope you have been able to start realizing how you have played a crucial role in the person you are today. I hope you have begun to crack the imposter mask that you have been wearing for years to allow space for the person you truly are.

Now, it's time to reclaim your life and thrive.

8.

Reclaim Your Life So You Can Thrive

"It's your reaction to adversity, not adversity itself that determines how your life's story will develop."

- Dieter F. Uchtdorf

B y now, you clearly understand how the beliefs we form in our subconscious play a role in how our lives unfold. If you don't, I did a very poor job with this book.

The Power of Beliefs

Questioning our beliefs in a world where everyone believes they are right can be challenging. I like to use the diet industry as an example of how we have an undeniable tendency to think that we are constantly correct (me included). As of now, there are no clear-cut studies that can say that one diet is better at losing weight than another. If we look into all the studies that have been done on each diet (keto, paleo, high carb/low fat, etc.), they all are found to be effective to some extent.

The problem is that not everyone who tries each diet

will lose weight. A trustable theory could be that we have different bodies, lifestyles, and genetic factors that make one universal diet complicated to achieve when losing weight. What works for me might not work for you.

So why do people keep fighting about this? Why can't we all agree that there is no such thing as one-size-fits-all in life?

The problem is that we tend to cling to our beliefs and think we are right, even if it means ignoring the evidence that proves us wrong. We also need to consider how our perception of situations plays a crucial role in what we believe. For example, if we have had negative experiences with a certain group of people, it may impact our beliefs about that group as a whole.

There is a very famous study that showed how our perception can be easily altered, known as the "broken windows theory." This theory suggests that a neighborhood with broken windows and signs of neglect will eventually lead to more crime because it sends the message that no one cares about the community. On the flip side, if a neighborhood is well-kept and has intact windows, it sends the message that the community is thriving and cared for.

Our perception of life can also impact our beliefs about ourselves. If we believe that we are not capable or deserving of success, it can hold us back from reaching our full potential. However, if we perceive ourselves as worthy and capable individuals, we are more likely to strive toward our goals and achieve them.

It is important to be aware of our perception and how it may affect our beliefs. We should consider different perspectives and always be open to new information and experiences that may challenge or change our beliefs. Only then can we have a more balanced and accurate understanding of the world around us.

It is important to constantly question our biases and perceptions to truly understand a situation and come to the most informed belief possible. By recognizing the impact of perception on our beliefs, we can become more open-minded and empathetic individuals.

It can be scary to question something that gives us structure and control in life, but it is necessary for growth. Challenging our beliefs means opening ourselves up to new information and experiences. It allows us to grow and adapt as individuals. So next time, before defending your beliefs with all your heart, take a step back and ask yourself if you are open to the possibility that you could be wrong.

And if not, maybe it's time to question why that is.

The Power of Balance

Balance. A very tough thing to achieve for me. I can confidently define myself as an extremist. Balance has never been my cup of tea. However, you have seen me write many times in this book about the importance of balance.

I have come to understand the power and importance of being balanced in all aspects of life.

Extremism can often lead us down a dangerous path, whether in our thoughts, emotions, or actions. Look at where it led me. It can blind us to other perspectives and solutions. It can lead to destructive behavior and hurt those around us. As I mentioned before, I do not think completely erasing imposter syndrome is helpful; the same goes for confidence, taking things personally, people pleasing, or self-doubt. If we had none, we would put ourselves in a situation with the possibility of significant failures. We would not be able to question our beliefs or listen to constructive criticism so we can adapt; we would not be able to grow. But if you find yourself in the other extremes, you also set yourself up for failure and unhappiness. I have learned that finding the correct balance is the key to success.

The stoic says not to let emotions rule our actions, but completely disregarding them is foolish. Emotions can provide valuable information and should be respected and acknowledged. But they should not be the sole drivers of our actions.

In our relationships with others, we must respect their boundaries and understand that everyone has a right to their own thoughts, feelings, and actions. But we also have the right to create and maintain boundaries for ourselves. We must find a balance between understanding and respecting others while also standing up for ourselves.

Balance is necessary for all aspects of life, and it is something that I continually work on every day.

Trust me, I am not saying it is an easy thing to do,

especially if, like me, you were not gifted with this natural ability to be balanced. But I have seen the positive effects it had on my life. Also, balance brings something very valuable, in my opinion: consistency. Every time we start something, whether it is starting our fitness journey or working on a project, we often hear that consistency is the key to success. We usually only see the success of someone and wrongly believe that it happened overnight when in fact, it was a long but consistent journey. We fail to see how this person has worked hard for years before having this "miraculously quick" success.

It is by consistently working on our project that success comes. However, when you are an extremist, working consistently can be challenging. When in the extremes, we often have plans or ideas that are too big and overwhelming to work on. We want to become Hulk in less than a month and therefore find ourselves going to the gym three hours per day and giving up quickly due to the unmanageable goal.

Success comes from finding balance, creating manageable plans, and being consistent.

So let us strive for balance in all aspects of our lives. Let us embrace moderation and reject extremism. The power of balance will bring us success, happiness, and a fulfilled life.

I encourage you to consider the power of balance in your own life and work toward achieving it.

The Power of Choices

Whether we like it or not, we all make choices. These choices, even the smallest ones, will impact the trajectory of our lives.

Even as small as it was, I made one choice that significantly impacted my life. On Friday, June 19, 2009, after the second day of our baccalaureate exam week, I ate a cheese panini for the first time. Stupid right? You wonder how a basic cheese panini could have affected the trajectory of my life. But trust me, it did.

The following day, I woke up in excruciating pain. Another acute pancreatitis attack had started. My father went into panic mode as it was clear that I would not be able to finish the most important exam of my scholastic career thus far. Without my baccalaureate, I would not be able to go to a university, and all the exams I had passed to enter business school would not change anything. Everything would fall apart because of my failure to obtain a high school diploma. In France, unlike in the United States, you only get your high school diploma if you pass the baccalaureate. The system is not based on continuous assessment.

I was screwed. Despite my father's perseverance to try to make the national education academy allow me to take the exam while in the hospital under morphine (yes, we did try that), they obviously refused, and I was left with no other choice than to try my luck at the makeup session in September.

I watched my friends celebrate their long-awaited baccalaureate and prepare for the next step of their life: college.

Even if I obtained my diploma in September, I would not be able to join a business school or university as the results would come at the end of September, later than the beginning of the school year. I would therefore lose one year just because I ate a cheese panini.

As I had missed three quarters of the year, my high school teachers advised that the best solution for me might be to redo one year. I reluctantly accepted, a hard choice to accept but a wise one.

The first day of school quickly arrived, and the reality of things hit me as I sat in the classroom as the only repeat student. I could not accept this fate. Repeating another year in high school while all my friends were already living college life was unbearable for me. Yes, I had missed a lot of school so repeating the year was warranted, but by deciding to opt out of the September exam, I was failing without even trying to get this diploma. And as I watched my new classmates, I made another choice. The one to go try my luck at the makeup session that started the following Monday.

The one-week exam was challenging. There, I met other students who had, like me, missed the June session due to health reasons for most. It was believed that because we had almost three additional months to study, the tests must be more complicated than the national June exam. I tried my best and hoped for success.

Two weeks later, I received the result. I failed. I obtained 9.84/20 when you need at least 10/20. Unlike the June exams, where an oral session was held for all students with more than 8/20, this was not the case for the September exam. I had to resign myself to the idea of accepting an extra year in high school.

The next day, I made another banal choice. I answered a landline call, something I had come to stop doing since the rise of the mobile phone. In the end, only solicitors were still calling on the landline. I cannot explain why I picked it up this time, and I am glad I did.

On the other line was one of the national education representatives. She told me that due to the very low success rate in the September baccalaureate exam (only three people passed out of 365 students in the Paris region), they had decided to organize the same makeup oral session as the one in June. It would be on Monday.

I was filled with joy as I started my express two-day preparations. I could do it; I had another chance.

And I did it. I obtained my diploma. I could not go to a university in France as the system does not allow it, but I quickly found a solution. A few months later, I flew to San Diego for a six-week long language course. These six weeks turned into six years.

So just because I ate a cheese panini, I went from desperation from being unable to pass my baccalaureate to failing it and ending up living in one of the best places on Earth (at least in my opinion).

Never underestimate the choices you make in your

life, as their impacts might be more significant than you think. And even when you feel that you might have made a wrong choice (like I believed with eating my cheese panini), it can bring you something you would never have expected.

Inaction is also a choice. By choosing not to act on something, you are making a choice. A choice that will impact you and only you. People often ask me, "How can you be so strong?" The answer is simple. I see it as a two-choice answer. I can decide to blame myself for everything that has happened or believe that life is unfair and that I did not deserve this. Or I can choose to try to do my best to manage my conditions, making it only possible to get better. It did not take me long to make my choice.

In the end, we are the only one living our life, so let's make it a good one.

The Power of Walking

I cannot write this book without discussing my best therapy and the tool that significantly contributed to successfully managing adversity: walking. I do not know what I would have done without walking. I know, people usually laugh when I tell them how incredibly powerful walking is. Even when I show them the countless research on the subject, they still do not want to believe it. They ask me: How do I have such a good memory? How do I have such a clear head during challenging times? How did

I become better at processing and controlling my emotions? The answer is walking.

It was in 2015 when I came across the benefit of walking. I was working for an event exhibition organizer, and we had our biggest conference in Cannes. Being in charge of all the VIP events meant I needed to walk between various venues on the Croisette. I was walking an average of 10 miles a day, and I was feeling better than ever. So when I returned to Paris and later arrived in Dubai, I kept up with this habit. I realized that walking was helping me be more in shape—mentally and physically. Still, most importantly, during my walks, I had my best ideas (yes, sometimes I do have good ideas!), especially those that require creativity. I was also able to process my emotions better. So I continue with the habit of going for a walk when I feel frustrated or angry or am working on a creative project.

When my prolapse came back after my first surgery, I was, as I said, devastated. I was on the edge as I was losing control and was faced with a situation where I could see no solution. It was hard, but I put on my sneakers and went for a power walk. As I started walking, I could not retain my tears, but I kept walking. And after 40 minutes, I slowly stopped crying, and my tears gave way to rage. Rage to fight and not to give up. When I returned home, I was in the correct mindset to manage whatever was coming my way.

And this is just one example. I can confidently say that walking has been a savior.

According to research, walking has proven to be beneficial for our brains, including improving memory and cognitive function, reducing stress and anxiety, and even increasing creativity. It also helps us process our emotions and strengthen our emotional regulation skills. When we walk, our body releases endorphins, improving our mood and decreasing stress levels.

There is a straightforward scientific explanation as to why walking allows these benefits. When we walk, our eyes absorb more information from our surroundings, stimulating the brain and improving neuronal connections. Our eyes shift rapidly from side to side to track the objects around us. These eye movements inhibit the amygdala, the brain region responsible for processing emotions such as stress, fear, and anxiety. When the amygdala is suppressed, negative emotions feel less intense, making us more able to separate our feelings from the situation that caused them. This makes it easier for us to process complex events and emotions.

Walking is also the root of a well-known therapy: eye movement desensitization and reprocessing (EMDR). Indeed, in the 1980s, American psychologist Francine Shapiro discovered the power of walking and eye movements in processing traumatic events. She developed EMDR, a therapy that combines guided imagery, breathing exercises, and bilateral stimulation (such as eye movements or tapping) to help clients process their traumatic experiences.

When facing difficult times, I often turn to walking as

my go-to therapy. It allows me to clear my head, process emotions, and come up with solutions to problems. I always encourage others to incorporate walking into their daily routine, even if it is just for a few minutes at a time. The benefits of walking for our brains and emotions are too valuable to ignore.

My tip is to start with 20 minutes, preferably in the morning, as it will allow your brain to see the sunlight (another powerful habit for your circadian rhythm) and make it fun by listening to your favorite podcast or calling a friend.

So go ahead and walk—your mind and body will thank you for it.

The Power of Nutrition

One thing I learned thanks to my diabetes and am the most grateful for is how much nutrition affects not only our body but also our mental state. I used to believe that food only affected my weight, while in fact, it involves much more than that.

One of the difficult things I had to do when I became diabetic was to question my core beliefs about nutrition. Over the years, I had built unfounded beliefs around food, and debunking them was not an easy task. I was one of these people who would start a juicing detox and so-called fast but with an effective diet like the cabbage soup one (if you have tried this one, cheers to you!) to "detox" my body. Of course, that was a lie. What I really wanted was to be thinner, as I thought my weight was the reason why I did not love myself. And like many people, I wanted things fast with lasting results, two things that usually do not go hand in hand.

So when I started to learn more about nutrition, I was shocked to learn how my actions were doing quite the opposite of what I had intended. In addition to causing my weight to yo-yo, I was killing my gut microbiome by starving my good bacteria that were in charge of many aspects of my brain functioning.

I first came across the gut-brain axis in 2020. This concept talks about the two-way communication between our gut and brain, including how the state of our gut microbiome can affect our mood and mental health. This means that what we eat not only impacts our physical health but also directly affects our brain function and overall well-being.

In addition, the gut produces around 90% of the body's serotonin, a key neurotransmitter involved in mood regulation. So let's say that from this day, I made sure to give my gut what it wanted.

So why do we often ignore the importance of food in our mental health treatment plans?

Research shows that certain probiotics can improve symptoms of depression and anxiety, while high sugar and processed diets have been linked to an increased risk for these disorders. The impact of sugar on my mood was something that became obvious thanks to my diabetes.

Now that I had data (my glucometer), I could see how high blood sugar correlated with higher anxiety.

But it doesn't stop there. Sugar can also disrupt normal brain function and impact essential neurotransmitters like dopamine and serotonin, leading to mood imbalances. Indeed, cutting out added sugars and focusing on whole, nutrient-dense foods was one of the most important steps I took in improving my mental health. Cutting sugary food is definitely not easy. The food industry made sure to include sugar in almost all processed foods, making it hard to avoid and causing addiction. But once you start reducing your sugar intake, you will feel the positive effects on both your physical and mental health.

In a study by Pano et al. (2021) that looked at the impact of nutrition on depression, they found that patients who followed a Mediterranean-style diet, rich in whole foods like fruits, vegetables, fish, and healthy fats, improved their symptoms significantly compared to those who didn't change their diets. I am not saying we should become obsessive about what we eat, as it adds another problem we do not need. Still, next time you find yourself with high levels of anxiety, check what your diet has been in the past few days and see if sugar might be the cause of this sudden, uncontrollable anxiety.

So let's prioritize nutrition in our journey toward better mental health and say "no" to added sugars. Your mind (and gut) will thank you.

The Power of Gratefulness

Once again, I will not lie: I was far from being a gratitude guru. Even if I felt grateful for the many things life brought me, I did not believe that being grateful impacted my happiness in life. When I was faced with countless studies on the matter, I started to open my eyes to its power.

What I came to learn is that gratefulness is not only about feeling grateful for the good things in your life but also acknowledging and accepting the challenges and difficulties. It allows us to appreciate what we have and shifts our focus from negative emotions such as resentment or envy.

Scientific studies have shown that incorporating gratefulness into daily life can result in higher happiness levels, better physical and psychological health, stronger relationships, and even improved sleep.

The benefits and importance of gratefulness are some of the first things you learn in positive psychology. And I found it to be true. To my friends and family's surprise, I am very grateful for everything that happened to me. I will always say that 2020 was one of the best years of my life. It allowed me to learn life lessons that people usually learn too late. During the toughest time, it was the small things that taught me to be grateful and helped me to move forward.

I learned to appreciate the small things and was so grateful when my best friends brought me a fruit cake for my birthday only a month after my diabetes diagnosis. I am still very grateful for all the friends who supported me when I needed support. I think I never realized how meaningful social connections and a community are in times of need.

With Aurore, it was love at first sight. Sometimes life puts people in your path that will come to have a great impact on your life, and she is one of them. I would not be the person I am today without her, and first and foremost, I might not have been here writing these words if we had not met.

I am grateful to have been living in Dubai during all these health challenges as I got access to the latest technology in the medical field and was able to get treated despite COVID-19, something that would not have been possible during this time in many countries.

The list of all the things I am grateful for could go on but listing all of them would make this one of the most boring books on Earth. You also have things—people, experiences, loved ones, pets, possessions, behaviors—to be grateful for and could fill your own personal, entire book. I think you get the point.

So I started to take a few minutes each day to reflect on the things I was grateful for. When I get angry about a situation where, to be honest, I should not, I think about how grateful I am to be in this position.

For example, some of us can react quickly in silly daily situations. I am ashamed to admit that I got mad at my Uber driver for taking the wrong way last time. I was late for a dinner, and making this small mistake led to an additional 10 minutes of drive time. It was nothing really, and when you write something like that down, you realize how foolish it is. Yes, I was going to be late, but at least I was going to have dinner in a restaurant, and I could go by car. Many people would die to be in this position. So after my irrational and inappropriate first reaction, I thought about how grateful I was and apologized to the driver.

We are so used to living our life that we forget how much we should be grateful for. When we grumble because the elevator does not come quickly, we do not think that at least we are lucky to have one. Of course, it is human to get mad sometimes for stupid things; we are imperfect beings. As seen previously, our brains tend to see the negative side of situations, making us forget about the positive details. But by remembering, even only occasionally, how lucky we are, we are much happier.

We should also learn to master our emotions. Mastering our emotions does not mean we should only allow positive emotions in our lives. On the contrary, the whole idea of mastering our emotions is centered around the philosophy that we should feel and acknowledge all emotions, but once felt, acknowledged, and understood, we should move on. Learn to ask yourself why you are feeling the emotion and if the emotion you're experiencing is masking your actual feelings. As we have seen before, we are experts at blinding ourselves sometimes.

Many people around me sympathized with how unlucky I was and how unfair it was that all these things happened to me. I think very differently about this. I am thankful for these experiences, for I have learned more about myself than I thought possible, and it allowed me to heal past trauma and thought patterns that prevented me from succeeding.

I don't wish my experiences on anyone, but my experiences taught me that life is very short and that we need to be aware of thought patterns that prevent us from living our lives to the fullest. I know now that I was never responsible for the genetic disease that my dad passed on to me and that the guilt I felt as a child led to me feeling like an imposter in my own life.

I also now realize that the only person who can change our life is us. We can learn something from all our experiences, and if we learn from them, even the most negative experience has value if we know how to perceive it. And I am grateful to have learned this lesson.

EPILOGUE

One morning as I was doing my routine power walk, I started to cry. I was not crying out of sadness but happiness. I could not retain my tears as I realized how happy I was. Finally, I was proud of who I was. I did not want to be anybody else. I could still see my many flaws, but I loved them. I was finally at peace with myself.

I wish everyone could live this moment at least once.

In writing this book, I wanted to share my own experience of how feeling like an imposter had a huge impact on my health and threatened my life at times. I realized during my research that I am not the only person to be affected by imposter syndrome and that the steps I took to free myself could be valuable to someone else as well.

During my battle with imposter syndrome, I discovered that my unconscious belief system was to blame for my falling victim to the syndrome. I had to challenge and question everything I believed about myself.

The consequences of imposter syndrome can be devastating, as I learned from my own experiences. It was a revelation to discover how feeling like an imposter can impact every sphere of your life, from your work, romantic relationships, and family relationships to friendships.

As I am wrapping up this book, my only hope is that you do not reach the same extent I did before taking action.

It is not your fault that you have developed this syndrome; however, it is your responsibility to manage it. Nobody is coming to fix you. And it is not their job to do so. If you do not realize that only you have the key to your life, you will be the one who will be penalized. We can spend years complaining and blaming ourselves or others for our lives when in fact, if we make the simple decision to act, we can, in less time, switch our lives around. Inaction is a choice. And our lives are a succession of choices.

Another point that I will repeat one last time, as it is by far the one that I believe will have the most impact on anybody's life, is that the quality of your life will depend on how you perceive and interpret situations. In all our experiences, we can interpret and emphasize the part of our choosing.

When many people saw my challenges as bad luck and misery, I did not. I didn't see how unlucky I was to have had sepsis, I saw how lucky I was to have survived and been given a second chance in life. When I was diagnosed with a genetic condition, I did not see the disadvantages thrown in my way but the perseverance and resilience I had gained. When I found out that I would not be able to have children, I was sad, but I was also so grateful to live in a city where I had access to the latest technology that gave me a solution to solve an issue that was preventing me from living as a normal person. The list can go on.

And if you take a deep look into your life, you too will be able to rewrite your story from a new point of view that will change how you see the world and how you approach it.

As I finish this book, I am now packed up, with my dead pancreas, my imperfections, my qualities, and my cooler filled with my medical supplies (thanks, YouTube!), ready to move to Lisbon, where a new journey awaits me. I am ready to close this chapter that brought me so much. Adversity might be coming again in my life, but I do not worry about it. Because now, I am confident that I will manage it to the best of my abilities. I will stand back up no matter what.

As you start your journey, I hope it will be as fulfilling as mine. Please don't blame yourself for the time it takes you to heal, as the result matters the most.

Many people think that pain or illness is the worst thing that can happen to you. I have experienced both, and for me, one of the worst things a human can experience is regret. Not letting regret consume you is difficult. Especially when your actions have caused you to lose so much. I thought I was invincible and denied the truth; I paid the price for it. Trust me; it is much easier to try not to have regrets instead. When you are on your deathbed, you will never regret trying, even if you failed. But you will regret anything you did not do because you were afraid of failing.

You only have one life, so you can either live it feeling like a fraud and never reach your full potential, or you can realize how your beliefs keep you in chains and take action to break free of them.

There is one game that you will only play once. That's life, so play it wisely. You are not an imposter, so start living your life to the fullest.

ACKNOWLEDGMENTS

During my journey, I was lucky to meet extraordinary individuals that have played a significant role in my health recovery and life.

I sincerely thank my medical team at Mediclinic Hospital for everything they have done for me: Dr. Al Hilou, Dr. Anastasios, Dr. Giaccaglia, Dr. Bhatti, and Dr. Gergy.

I want to thank my family for their love and support in my life.

I am grateful to my editor, Quinn, whose unwavering support and encouragement have empowered me to write this book.

I want to thank all my friends who have supported me in sickness and health.

I want to thank my wonderful co-workers who have supported me in times of need. I want to thank Tifanie personally, who had to endure my obsession with my blood sugar (and many more things!), and Marine, without whom I might not be living my dream today.

I want to thank all my teachers at the University of Louisiana at Monroe, from whom I have learned much.

I want to thank all my teachers at *The Platform*

Studios for teaching me how exercise can bring much more than a fit body.

I want to thank all the individuals who share their knowledge with the world, without whom I would not have been able to learn as much as I did.

I have included on the book website the most valuable resources I came across during my journey.

ADDITIONAL RESSOURCES

On the journey to success, knowledge is power.
To help you discover invaluable resources that have helped
me during my journey, visit our website and explore the
carefully crafted list I have created.

www.youarenotanimposter.com

END NOTES

Introduction

American Psychological Association. (n.d.). Imposter phenomenon. In *American Psychological Association.org dictionary*. https://dictio nary.apa.org/impostor-phenomenon

Clance, P. R., & Imes, S. A. (1978). The imposter phenomenon in high achieving women: Dynamics and therapeutic intervention. *Psychotherapy: Theory, Research & Practice, 15*(3), 241-247. https://psycnet.apa.org/record/1979-26502-001

Langford, J., & Clance, P. R. (1993). The impostor phenomenon: Recent research findings regarding dynamics, personality and family patterns and their implications for treatment. Psychotherapy: Theory, Research & Practice, *30*(3), 495-501. doi:10.1037/0033-3204.30.3.495.

Robinson, A. (2017). *Overcoming imposter syndrome: How to stop feeling like a fraud*. Psychopharmacology and Substance Abuse. https://www.apadivisions.org/division-28/publications/newslet ters/psychopharmacology/2017/11/imposter-syndrome

Chapter 1

American Psychological Association. (2012). *What you need to know about willpower: The psychological science of self-control*. American Psychological Association. https://www.apa.org/topics/personal ity/willpower

Arain, M., Haque, M., Johal, L., Mathur, P., Nel, W., Rais, A., Sandhu, R., & Sharma, S. (2013). Maturation of the adolescent brain. *Neuropsychiatric Disease and Treatment, 9*, 449-461. https://www.ncbi.nlm.nih.gov/pmc/articles/
PMC3621648/#:~:text=The%20development%20and%20matura-

tion%20of%20the%20prefrontal%20cortex%20occurs%20primari-ly,helps%20accomplish%20executive%20brain%20functions

Clark, M. A. (2016, April 1). *Workaholism: It's not just long hours of work*. American Psychological Association. https://www.apa.org/science/about/psa/2016/04/workaholism#:~:text=The%20term%20workaholism%20was%20coined

Dow, M. (2019). *Your subconscious brain can change your life: Overcome obstacles, heal your body, and reach any goal with a revolutionary technique*. Hay House Inc.

Dutheil, F., Charkhabi, M., Ravoux, H., Brousse, G., Dewavrin, S., Cornet, T., Mondillon, L., Han, S., Pfabigan, D., Baker, J. S., Mermillod, M., Schmidt, J., Moustafa, F., & Pereira, B. (2020). Exploring the link between work addiction risk and health-related outcomes using job-demand-control model. *International Journal of Environmental Research and Public Health, 17*(20), 7594. https://doi.org/10.3390/ijerph17207594

Eurich, T. (2018, October 19). *Working with people who aren't self-aware*. Harvard Business Review. https://hbr.org/2018/10/working-with-people-who-arent-self-aware

Eurodoc Equality Working Group. (2020, December 1). *Overworking, impostor syndrome, and ableism: A reflection on "normality" in Academia*. Eurodoc. http://eurodoc.net/news/2020/overworking-impostor-syndrome-and-ableism-a-reflection-on-normality-in-academia

Fuerte, K. (2021, July 6). *The "Karoshi" phenomenon is now a worldwide problem*. Observatory Institute for the Future of Education. https://observatory.tec.mx/edu-news/karoshi-phenomenon

Lamla, M. C. (2011, April 4). *Shame: A concealed, contagious, and dangerous emotion*. Psychology Today. https://www.psychologytoday.com/us/blog/intense-emotions-and-strong-feelings/201104/shame-concealed-contagious-and-dangerous-emotion

Martin, S. M. (2018, May 25). *Don't rely on others to validate your feelings*. PsychCentral. https://psychcentral.com/blog/imperfect/2018/05/dont-rely-on-others-to-validate-your-feelings

O'Connor, P. (2014, May 9). *What's wrong with 'rock bottom.'*

Psychology Today. https://www.psychologytoday.com/us/blog/philosophy-stirred-not-shaken/201405/whats-wrong-rock-bottom

Strauss Cohen, I. (2017, December 26). *The benefits of delaying gratification*. Psychology Today. https://www.psychologytoday.com/us/blog/your-emotional-meter/201712/the-benefits-delaying-gratification

Chapter 2

Berry, W. (2020, May 19). *How to control your mind*. Psychology Today. https://www.psychologytoday.com/us/blog/the-second-noble-truth/202005/how-control-your-mind

Dow, M. (2019). *Your subconscious brain can change your life: Overcome obstacles, heal your body, and reach any goal with a revolutionary technique*. Hay House.

Getting to equal: Career confidence and the path to leadership. (2019). Ecompass equality. https://www.encompassequality.com/research-2019

Kahneman, D. (2011). *Thinking, fast and slow*. Farrar, Straus and Giroux.

Michalak, K. (n.d.). *Schema*. Britannica. https://www.britannica.com/science/schema-cognitive

Moukheiber, A. (2022). *Your brain is playing tricks on you: How the brain shapes opinions and perceptions*. Hero.

Parvez, H. (2021, May 18). *How our past experiences shape our personality*. PsychMechanics. https://www.psychmechanics.com/how-our-past-experiences-shape-our/

Sonnak, C., & Towell, T. (2001). The impostor phenomenon in British university students: Relationships between self-esteem, mental health, parental rearing style and socioeconomic status. *Personality and Individual Differences, 31*(6), 863-874. https://doi.org/10.1016/s0191-8869(00)00184-7

Young, V. (2011). *The secret thoughts of successful women: Why capable people suffer from the impostor syndrome and how to thrive in spite of it*. Crown Business.

Chapter 3

Blakely, S. (2022, March 18). *Finding your purpose*. MasterClass. https://www.masterclass.com/classes/sara-blakely-teaches-self-made-entrepreneurship/chapters/finding-your-purpose?action=preview&controller=chapters&course_id=sara-blakely-teaches-self-made-entrepreneurship&id=finding-your-purpose&logged_in=true

Brown, A. (2022, September 29). *42 factors that affect blood glucose?! A surprising update*. diaTribe. https://diatribe.org/42-factors-affect-blood-glucose-surprising-update

Dizikes, P. (2022, April 22). *Study finds an unexpected upside to workplace impostor thoughts*. Massachusetts Institute of Technology. https://news.mit.edu/2022/imposter-syndrome-upside-0415

Gilbert, E. (2015). *Big magic: Creative living beyond fear*. Riverhead Books.

Gilbert, E. (2019, August 15). *Let's call perfectionism what it really is* [Video]. Youtube. https://www.youtube.com/watch?v=NlLyeozPmOs

Goler, L., Gale, J., Harrington, B., & Grant, A. (2018, January 11). *Why people really quit their jobs*. Harvard Business Review. https://hbr.org/2018/01/why-people-really-quit-their-jobs

Kelland, M. (n.d.). *Personality theory in a cultural context*. OpenStax CNX. http://cnx.org/content/col11901/1.1/

Martin, S. (2015, December 8). *What causes perfectionism?* PsychCentral. https://psychcentral.com/blog/imperfect/2015/12/what-causes-perfectionism#1

Tiwari, S. C. (2013). Loneliness: A disease? *Indian journal of psychiatry, 55*(4), 320-322. https://www.ncbi.nlm.nih.gov/pmc/articles/PMC3890922/

Voss, C., & Raz, T. (2016). *Never split the difference: Negotiating as if your life depended on it*. HarperBusiness.

Chapter 4

Baumeister, R. F., DeWall, C. N., Ciarocco, N. J., & Twenge, J. M. (2005). Social exclusion impairs self-regulation. *Journal of Personality and Social Psychology, 88*(4), 589-604. https://pubmed.ncbi. nlm.nih.gov/15796662/

Carnegie, D. (1998). *How to stop worrying and start living.* Simon & Schuster.

Dwyer, D. J. (2018, March 28). *Why approval-holics are so afraid.* Psychology Today. https://www.psychologytoday.com/us/blog/ got-minute/201803/why-approval-holics-are-so-afraid

Ehring, T. (2021). Thinking too much: Rumination and psychopathology. *World Psychiatry, 20*(3), 441-442. https://doi.org/10.1002/ wps.20910

Imbo, F. (2020, March 4). *How not to take things personally?* [Address]. TEDxMechelen. https://www.youtube.com/watch?v=LnJw H_PZXnM&t=19s.

Ito, T. A., Larsen, J. T., Smith, N. K., & Cacioppo, J. T. (1998). Negative information weighs more heavily on the brain: The negativity bias in evaluative categorizations. *Journal of Personality and Social Psychology, 75*(4), 887-900. https://pubmed.ncbi.nlm.nih.gov/ 9825526/

Kross, E., Bruehlman-Senecal, E., Park, J., Burson, A., Dougherty, A., Shablack, H., Bremner, R., Moser, J. & Ayduk, O. (2014). Self-talk as a regulatory mechanism: How you do it matters. *Journal of Personality and Social Psychology, 106*(2), 302-324. https:// pubmed.ncbi.nlm.nih.gov/24467424/

Lieberman, M. D., Eisenberger, N. I., Crockett, M. J., Tom, S. M., Pfeifer, J. H., & Way, B. M. (2007). Putting feelings into words: Affect labeling disrupts amygdala activity in response to affective stimuli. *Psychological Science, 18*(5), 421-428. https://pubmed.ncbi. nlm.nih.gov/17576282/#:~:text=The%20results%20indicated%20that%20affect,ventrolateral%20prefrontal%20cortex%20

Metrinko, L. (2020, July 30). *7 dangerous effects of overthinking.* Psych2Go. https://psych2go.net/7-dangerous-effects-of- overthinking/

Rankin, L. (2015). *Mind over medicine: Scientific proof that you can heal yourself.* Hay House.

Sanderson, C. A. (2019, September 23). *How to prime your mind for optimism.* Greater Good Magazine. https://greatergood.berkeley. edu/article/item/how_to_prime_your_mind_for_optimism

Sharot, T., Riccardi, A. M., Raio, C. M., & Phelps, E. A. (2007). Neural mechanisms mediating optimism bias. *Nature, 450,* 102-105. https://www.nature.com/articles/nature06280

Tolle, E. (2004). *The power of now: A guide to spiritual enlightenment.* New World Library.

Van Edwards, V. (2017). *Captivate: The science of succeeding with people.* Portfolio.

Weir, K. (2012). The pain of social rejection. *Monitor on Psychology, 43*(4), 50. https://www.apa.org/monitor/2012/04/ rejection#:~:text=%E2%80%9CHumans%20have%20a%20funda- mental%20need,at%20the%20University%20of%20Kentucky

What is a people pleaser? (2021, October 25). WebMD. https://www. webmd.com/mental-health/what-is-a-people-pleaser

Chapter 5

Moore, C. (2022, September 12). *Positive daily affirmations: Is there science behind it?* PositivePsychology.com. https://positivepsychol ogy.com/daily-affirmations/

Peer, M. (2009). *Ultimate confidence: The secrets to feeling great about yourself every day.* Sphere.

Warrell, M. (2017, December 11). *How to beat self-doubt and stop selling yourself short.* Forbes. https://www.forbes.com/sites/margiewarrell/ 2017/12/09/doubt-your-doubts/?sh=1416cc7b151a

Chapter 6

Byerly, T. R., Hill, P. C., & Edwards, K. J. (2022). Others-centeredness: A uniquely positive tendency to put others fist. *Personality and*

Individual Differences, 189(Part A), 111364. https://www.sciencedirect.com/science/article/abs/pii/S0191886921007431

Leonard, E. (2020, November 23). *The underpinnings of people-pleasing.* Psychology Today. https://www.psychologytoday.com/us/blog/peaceful-parenting/202011/the-underpinnings-people-pleasing

Perel, E. (n.d.). Esther Perel. https://www.estherperel.com/

The subtle effects of trauma: People pleasing. (2021, January 8). Khiron Clinics. https://khironclinics.com/blog/people-pleasing/

Van Edwards, V. (2017). *Captivate: The science of succeeding with people.* Portfolio.

Chapter 7

Duckworth, A. (2016). *Grit: The power of passion and perseverance.* Collins.

Dweck, C. (2006). *Mindset: The new psychology of success.* Random House.

Gladwell, M. (2011). *Outliers: The story of success.* Back Bay Books.

Housel, M. (2020). *The psychology of money: Timeless lessons on wealth, greed, and happiness.* Harriman House.

Huberman, A. (Host). (2022, January 17). The science of setting & achieving goals (No. 55) [Audio podcast episode]. In *Huberman Lab.* Huberman Lab Scicomm Media. https://hubermanlab.com/the-science-of-setting-and-achieving-goals/

Kahneman, D. (2011). *Thinking, fast and slow.* Farrar, Straus and Giroux.

Pluchino, A., Biondo, A. E., & Rapisarda, A. (2018). Talent versus luck: The role of randomness in success and failure. *Advances in Complex Systems, 21*(3 & 4). https://www.worldscientific.com/doi/pdf/10.1142/S0219525918500145

Van Edwards, Vanessa. (2022, July 19). *What to say when someone compliments you... and keep it non-awkward* [Video]. Youtube. https://www.youtube.com/watch?v=0E80D3pAt6c

Chapter 8

Bem, D. (1972). Self-perception theory. *Advances in Experiment Social Psychology*, *6*, 1-62. https://www.researchgate.net/publication/277682193_Self-Perception_Theory

Emmons, R. A., & Mishra, A. (2011). Why gratitude enhances well-being: What we know, what we need to know. *Designing Positive Psychology: Taking Stock and Moving Forward*, 248-262. https://academic.oup.com/book/4376/chapter-abstract/146327521?redirectedFrom=fulltext&login=false

Gomez-Pinilla, F. & Hillman, C. (2013). The influence of exercise on cognitive abilities. *Comprehensive Physiology*, *3*(1), 403-428. https://pubmed.ncbi.nlm.nih.gov/23720292/

Palfreman, J. (Writer & Director). (2004, April 8). Diet wars (Season 22, Episode 7) [TV series episode]. In J. Palfreman, M. Sullivan, & D. Fanning (Executive Producers), *Frontline*. Palfreman Film Group; WGBH Boston, https://www.pbs.org/wgbh/pages/frontline/shows/diet/etc/script.html

Pano, O., Martínez-Lapiscina, E. H., Sayón-Orea, C., Martinez-Gonzalez, M. A., Martinez, J. A., & Sanchez-Villegas, A. (2021). Healthy Diet, depression and quality of life: A narrative review of biological mechanisms and primary prevention opportunities. *World Journal of Psychiatry*, *11*(11), 997-1016. https://www.ncbi.nlm.nih.gov/pmc/articles/PMC8613751/

Ruhl, C. (2021, July 26). *The broken windows theory*. Simply Psychology. https://www.simplypsychology.org/broken-windows-theory.html

Samiento, M. (2020, June 8). *Addressing unconscious bias: Where awareness and understanding begin*. Nonprofit Leadership Center. https://nlctb.org/tips/unconscious-bias/

Shapiro, F. (1989). Efficacy of the eye movement desensitization procedure in the treatment of traumatic memories. *Journal of Traumatic Stress, 2*(2), 199-223.

Šimić, G., Tkalčić, M., Vukić, V., Mulc, D., Španić, E., Šagud, M., Olucha-Bordonau, F. E., Vukšić, M., Hof, P. R. (2021). Understanding emotions: Origins and roles of the amygdala. *Biomolecules,* *11*(6), 823. https://www.mdpi.com/2218-273X/11/6/823

Venegas-Sanabria, L. C., Martínez-Vizcaino, V., Cavero-Redondo, I., Chavarro-Carvajal, D. A., Cano-Gutierrez, C. A., & Álvarez-Bueno, C. (2021). Effect of physical activity on cognitive domains in dementia and mild cognitive impairment: Overview of systematic reviews and meta-analyses. *Aging & Mental Health, 25*(11), 1977-1985. https://pubmed.ncbi.nlm.nih.gov/33143444/

Index

D

N

name written on a stone xviii
natural ability 179
natural tendencies 21
naturally optimistic 120
navigate the world 26, 38
negative
  experiences 37, 176
  health effects. 86
  self-image 30
  bias 92-93
neural pathways 95-96
neurological level 169
neuronal connections 185
neuroscience 20, 92
neurotic tendencies 145
neuroticism 146
neurotransmitter 187
Never Split the Difference 54
new neural pathways 95-96
new resolution 2
nightmare 77
Nobel prize 38
non-diabetic line 46, 76
nonnegotiable fee 118
normal behavior xv
nurses 5, 20

O

obsessive person 77
offspring 73
open-minded 177
operating theater 20
organizational psychologists 68
Overthinking 102, 166
overworking 12-13, 15, 119
Own Your Successes 155, 159, 161, 163, 165, 167, 169, 171

P

pain-free 44
painkillers 5
Pakistan 3
Paleo 175

pancreas 42, 44-45, 48, 112, 115, 123, 195
pancreatitis 35, 42, 44, 46, 115, 180
Pancreatogenic Diabetes 48
panic mode 11, 180
Pano 188
Paperwork 136, 138
paralyzed in fear 5
Paris 143, 182, 184
part of the spectrum 109
partner's actions 75
path of recovery 47
Pauline Rose Clance xiv
peace xviii, 193
people pleaser 2, 29, 119, 134, 140, 145
People Pleasing Can Be Rooted in 143
people with disabilities 31
people-pleasing attitude 136
people-pleasing habit 153
Perel 142
perfect lives 55-56, 58
Perfection Is the Only Option 60
perfectionism 19, 28, 40, 53-55, 58, 60-61, 63-68, 72-80
Perfectionism in Place of Love 66
perfectionists 12, 70-71
perseverance 5, 158, 164, 170, 180, 195
personal attack 98
personal development 10
Pets 190
physical pain 90
physiological response 86, 89
piece of cake 76
pieces of the puzzle 120, 123
Pluchino 158
popping something out of a box xix
positive
  affirmations 120-121
  changes 10, 21
  effects 77, 179, 188
power walk 184
Practice mindfulness 10
prefrontal cortex 21, 97
pressure of social norms xvi
primitive mechanism 86
probiotics 187
problems in relationships 8
professional scam artist 138
professional settings xiv

ABOUT THE AUTHOR

Coline Monsarrat is passionate about helping others overcome obstacles and fostering self-awareness for personal growth.

Born with a genetic disease, she has faced her fair share of challenges, which have shaped her perspective on thriving. Determined to empower others, she wrote her book as a guide to understanding the barriers that hinder personal progress. Through her work, Coline emphasizes the importance of self-awareness as a catalyst for growth.

With a Bachelor's degree in Psychology from the University of Louisiana at Monroe, Coline initially pursued a career in the global luxury perfume industry. However, her longing for a more meaningful vocation led her to embark on a journey to make a positive impact on young minds.

Currently residing in the beautiful city of Lisbon, Coline dedicates herself to writing the next exciting adventure in her middle-grade book series, Aria & Liam. Launched in 2022, this series has captured the hearts of young readers, providing them with relatable characters and thought-provoking storytelling.